Can You Hear Me Now?

Applying Brain Research and Technology to Engage Today's Students

Authors

Jerry Michel

Lisa Nimz

Foreword

LaVonna Roth, M.S.Ed.

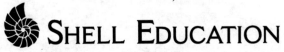

SHELL EDUCATION

Publishing Credits

Dona Herweck Rice, *Editor-in-Chief;* Lee Aucoin, *Creative Director;*
Robin Erickson, *Production Director;* Timothy J. Bradley, *Illustration Manager;*
Sara Johnson, M.S.Ed., *Senior Editor;* Evelyn Garcia, *Associate Education Editor;*
Juan Chavolla, *Cover and Interior Layout Designer;* Tim Bradley, *Illustrator;*
Corinne Burton, M.A.Ed., *Publisher*

JBM: for Mama, Papa, KT, and Bella for letting me be.

LBN: To the strong women in my life—my mother, Diana and my partner Kim. I'd be lost without you.

Shell Education

5301 Oceanus Drive
Huntington Beach, CA 92649-1030
http://www.shelleducation.com

ISBN 978-1-4258-0846-4

©2012 Shell Educational Publishing, Inc.

Table of Contents

Foreword

Dear Friends in Education,

As the scientific worlds of technology and brain research evolve in understanding, we are exposed to more and more ways learning can be affected. Technology offers a vast variety of ways to share content with students—such as the use of a document camera that shows a living species in a Petri dish to online video chatting with students in another country who share information about their culture and geography in real time. The opportunities are endless, and we must take advantage of them since this is the world we live in and the skills required for the 21st century are interwoven with it.

At the same time, we must move cautiously forward in making assumptions. Although major discoveries in brain research have been made through the use of ever-improving technology, we must be careful not to assume one discovery or one study directly relates to what must happen in the classroom. We must be aware of how many times something has occurred and over what length of time. Thus, what we can do is take a look at the educational implications and use that knowledge with our own action research in the classroom to make determinations on what is improving student learning—thus achievement. We know that neuroplasticity, as well as neurogenesis, are foundational keys to the brain and how it learns. However, many educators are unaware of these terms and the integral part they play in our classrooms and student achievement. As you read through *Can You Hear Me Now?: Applying Brain Research and Technology to Engage Today's Students*, pay careful attention to the fact that the brain does change, for the positive or negative, and things can be done in classrooms to foster this change in ways that challenge, outside negative circumstances.

One of the greatest struggles teachers face today is getting students involved in their learning. Students often lack motivation, excitement, ownership, and seeing the relevancy of the content in their own lives. Although these conditions are often true, they differ classroom-to-classroom and teacher-to-teacher. The authors of this book, Jerry Michel and Lisa Nimz, provide educators with insight into the importance of overcoming these obstacles. They share ruminations—examples and insights that open educator's eyes to the importance of change. Changing with the times of new discoveries. Changing with our understanding of brain research and powerful insights. Changing based on opportunities that technology provides us. Changing to do what we must for our students and our future. Can we hear them? Are we listening? It's time.

Thank you, Jerry and Lisa, for giving educators insight into the importance of technology and brain research. Most importantly, thank you for doing it in a way that allows educators to connect what is shared here to guide their teaching and to watch more closely what happens in their classroom "laboratories."

—LaVonna Roth, M.S.Ed, M.A.T.
Author of *Brain-Powered Strategies to Engage All Learners*

Acknowledgements

We are grateful to Dona Rice for seeing the nascent book behind our IRA presentation and to Sara Johnson for helping us shape the concept into a manuscript. Many thanks to Joan Irwin for her insight and thoughtful editing, and to Evelyn Garcia for bringing it home. And thanks to the folks behind Google Docs™, whoever you are, for making such a fun and effective way to collaborate in the cloud.

—Jerry and Lisa

Who knew this journey would start with some musings about mirror neurons and how they influence the way we read and learn? We have explored the science behind learning and literacy development in classrooms, at workshops, while giving presentations, through text messages, in chatrooms, in the stacks of Skokie Public Library, a stray coffeehouse or two, and over more meals than we can count. All those places were full of people whose encouragement makes the struggle of writing, revising, and sharing worth all the headaches, including: the readers and writers from Room 5 at Devonshire School; the middle schoolers at Lincoln Hall who kept me from becoming a fossil; all the Willard kids who make learning a hoot; my teaching friends and colleagues from Skokie, Lincolnwood, and Evanston—I continue to be inspired by some of the best educators in the schools today; and, most importantly, to Lisa, who let me wander without getting too lost, for being the science behind my shovel, and for making sure that no idea was left behind.

—Jerry Michel

I am grateful to: Jerry for some of the best food, beverages, and ideas I have ever known; the Skokie District 68 community and families who have so deeply enhanced my life; Sue O'Neil whose leadership and compassion have made Jane Stenson School a premier place to teach and learn, and whose expertise and insight have helped me become a better teacher; and my home biscuits at Stenson for the support and the humor that make me glad to come to work. I am inspired by the quiet, unassuming mastery of the art and craft of teaching in our building; the 4Nsters and 5Nsters throughout the years; the students who have been my teachers; my dad for his enthusiastic support and pride in me; my brother for lending me his strong backbone when mine felt soft; Janet and Chelle for their enduring friendship; my mom for the talking, the thinking, the being, and so much more than I am able to express here; and I am especially grateful to Kim, Jessie, and Maya for the ways in which we share our lives. I simply lahhhve you, dahlings.

—Lisa Nimz

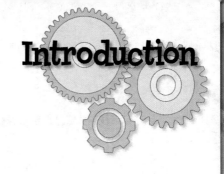

Ruminations

After reading "Which brain research can educators trust?" (Willis 2007), Lisa sent a message to the author and Willis included it in a subsequent article (2008). Lisa wrote:

"We know how important it is for relevant research from the scientific community to be shared with and used in the education community. We are anxious for neurological research to become more a part of educators' thinking and wonder how to make it so. There seem to be only a few people in the unique position of being able to understand the research, figure out its implications for the classroom, and use those implications to direct their teaching. We are actively pondering how a sturdy and wide enough bridge can be built between the scientific community and the education community.

"There are many obstacles to building such a construct. Reading the primary sources of neurological research can be challenging even for the brightest of us. And even if someone can comprehend these primary sources, there are many highly educated people who don't seem to approach scientific evidence with the caution and skepticism necessary to make fair judgments about the implications of that evidence. There are also many members of the scientific community and academia who haven't studied pedagogy. We are thankful for books, articles, and presentations that mitigate some of that disconnect."

Navigating a 2.0 Landscape

Our passion for teaching and learning inspired us to write this book to demonstrate how we have made connections between findings from neuroscience, our knowledge of pedagogy, and the impact of technology on teaching and learning. We, like many others in education, often find ourselves in a quandary about how best to interpret scientific findings about how the brain learns, and then apply these findings to what we do in our classrooms.

Unparalleled advances in brain research are taking place today. Through this research, we are coming to understand that our brains have greater learning and growth potential than we realized. It is the perfect storm: while neuroscience teaches us about our potential, advances in technology feed that potential with the world's collective expertise. We are truly living in a golden age of learning. This age is characterized by technological resources that are readily accessible to the majority of our students. Creating learning environments that capitalize on available digital tools which advance learning and sustain students' motivation is a challenge confronting teachers at all levels.

Educators and students occupy the same rooms in the same buildings, but at times it seems as if they are living in separate worlds. To be an educator is to be an ambassador from academe—the world of study and knowledge. Schools can be thought of granting children tourist visas, but the aim of schooling is to make sure they acquire their own citizenship. Schools are designed to enable students to become lifelong learners.

The students with whom educators share their physical spaces are growing up in a digital world. Often times they are alone at their computers or with their handheld devices, creating, transmitting, and receiving information. They are able to quickly make more connections today compared to any other time in our history. Facts and figures, family and friends, full-length novels, and thirty-second videos are all at their fingertips for their instant consideration and consumption. Rosen (2010) observes that children born in the 1990s and the new millennium are more enmeshed in technology than their predecessors, and are able to capitalize on innovations that now seem to be almost daily occurrences. Rosen uses the term *iGeneration* to define these students, noting "it is the iGeneration student's love of all things technological that needs to be incorporated in the way we teach them in and out of the classroom" (2010, 16).

Like Rosen, we believe that 21st century educators must do more than acknowledge the parallel existence of academe and cyberspace, while taking care to avoid the allure of thinking that today's students are somehow hardwired differently than previous generations. We must find the places where students' digital lives can intersect with instructional goals, and then meet our students there in order to adequately teach and learn. Rather than eschewing new media and technology for fear that it competes with literacy development, we must use these tools to enhance student learning.

Any useful instructional tool should be multipurpose, and classroom technology should be much more than just another way to play "classroom jeopardy." One of Lisa's colleagues wondered if students would find mathematics more meaningful if the numbers and operations they were learning also held some kind of personal context for them. Lisa then created a wiki in which she and her colleague asked students to post real-life mathematical problems. Once the problems were online, they asked the students to choose one to solve and email the answer to the classmate who wrote it. Another colleague of Lisa's realized that students wrote better essays for their philosophy unit if they were aware of their classmates' reactions to philosophical questions. Each student responded to the questions in a wiki, and the classmates were easily able to share their ideas.

Students can even use these tools to generate their own activities. Jerry knows a third-grader who made a podcast of the times tables. She read the problem, paused, and gave the answer. On her way to soccer, she listened to the podcast and practiced, giving the answer in the pauses. Schoolwork presented in the traditional manner is not always engaging for students. But if the schoolwork is intertwined with today's technology, it can make a difference in the classroom.

Another advantage of these tools is that they make it easier for students to have a voice in their own learning path. As you will see in the upcoming chapters, teachers will be given options that they make it easier to find out what students need to help their comprehension and interest levels, and to then differentiate instruction according to those needs. Allowing students to have a voice, a choice, and opportunities to join you in making instructional decisions is crucial in motivating them. Such opportunities acknowledge their goals and their hopes, and help them feel like they are an important factor in the learning equation. In a lecture given in 1995, Dr. James Comer first shared the idea that has resonated with many educators and researchers since: No significant learning occurs without a significant relationship. That relationship occurs when both sides are allowed to make a contribution. Research has shown that positive relationships between teachers and students are important factors in effective instruction. Marzano notes: "Perhaps the most powerful message from research is that relationships are a matter of student perception. They have little to do with how a teacher actually feels about students; it's what teachers do that dictates how students perceive those relationships" (2011, 82).

However, in the 21st century, relationships are not enough. Educators must develop these relationships while also being mindful of how data analysis, differentiation, and accessibility to curriculum standards play a role in making these relationships significant for all students. As educators search for the intersections between the academic world and student lives, trust is built by cultivating positive student-teacher relationships as well as by creating successful student-curriculum connections. Undoubtedly, technology and social media will play a significant role in how these connections form for students, both in and out of future classrooms. This context is similar to coaching beginning athletes and musicians; while it is important to make the practice enjoyable, it is equally important to help them remember how pleasing it is to compete and perform successfully in a game or concert.

Our Perspective

In downtown Winnipeg, Manitoba, Canada, sits a picturesque marina the locals call The Forks. For close to 6,000 years, this site has served as a meeting place for generations of people,—from the First Nations peoples who originally travelled in the area, to the traders, immigrants, and current-day tourists who visit there today. The Forks is special because it is at the confluence of the Red and Assiniboine Rivers.

Like the confluence of the major rivers, the influx of technology and social media may be viewed as a torrent of information moving too quickly to process. But viewed within the framework of cognitive science, we take a view similar to that of the throngs of people at The Forks. We see our current time as a unique space: a historical convergence of technology and brain research that will lead to a renaissance in education.

Cognitive science—a nexus between neuroscience, computer science, psychology, and anthropology—reveals that the skills students need in order to function in the 21st century are not necessarily new (Rotherham and Willingham 2009). Like students in the past, students of today must learn how to solve problems, work collaboratively, think critically, and make purposeful choices (Knobel and Lankshear 2006). What differs between the generations is the context that technology now inhabits. Students' access to, and expectations for using digital tools outside and within schools is greater than before. Despite the ever-present new media and social learning networks, the focus of this book is how educators can effectively deliver instruction that maximizes students' ability to grow emotionally, academically, and metacognitively through the effective use of digital resources. Our perspective is consistent with concepts defined in the NMC Horizon Report: 2011 K–12 Edition, notably that "sense-making and the ability to assess the credibility of information are paramount," and "digital literacy is less about tools and more about thinking" (Johnson, Adams, and Haywood 2011, 4–5).

Neuroscientists have learned more about the workings of the human brain in the last four decades than in the last two millennia; the number of books and research articles has exploded (Sousa 2010). Educational neuroscience is an emerging field which takes into account findings from psychology, pedagogy, and neuroscience (Samuels 2009). Sousa illustrates the interactions among these disciplines in the diagram below.

Fig. 1. The emergence of educational neuroscience at the intersection of psychology, neuroscience, and pedagogy

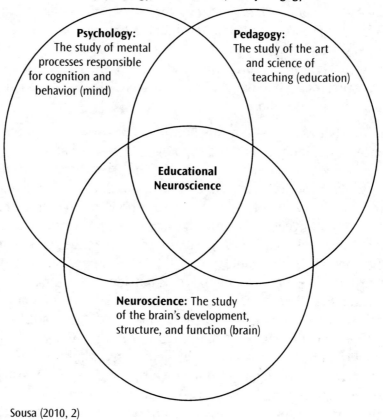

Sousa (2010, 2)

Discoveries from brain research have provided additional insights into factors that contribute to effective teaching and learning. Willis (2008; 2010) contends that research can indicate the most appropriate emotional, cognitive, and social environments for learning, and educators can use knowledge of how the brain works to "guide the strategies, curriculum, and interventions they select for specific goals and individual students" (2010, 47).

Some of the major findings of brain research that have influenced our thinking about teaching and learning include:

- Brain plasticity enables the formation of new neural networks meaning that the brain can rewire itself.
- Giftedness and talent can be developed and are not innate as once thought to be.
- Emotions have a great impact on learning.
- The school's social and emotional climate affects learning.
- Incremental, achievable challenges matched to students' level of ability sustain interest and motivation.
- Students' collaborative role in learning is crucial.

The latter point is particularly compelling for teachers. Children do not learn to their fullest potential nor are they engaged at the highest levels when we merely tell them what they need to know. Learners of all ages have always been more easily engaged when they are presented with a mental challenge that is demanding without being baffling. And they are more engaged when they know why something is important to learn. We have developed this book to provide guidance to educators and help them use the exciting technologies that inspire students as well as enabling them to aspire to important goals.

Being a successful educator depends squarely on adopting a growth mindset (Dweck 2010). If one of the primary goals of education is to help students develop into lifelong learners, teachers must take every opportunity to model their own learning. Teachers and students can collaborate in both teaching and learning. The resources and strategies that we present in this book can be an integral part of this process.

With all of the exciting novelty of technology and its gadgets, it is important for educators to realize that technology should not be an event; instead, it is as central to today's students as the stylus and tablet were for the first scribes. Technology is not the nemesis of literacy and numeracy, but a means to develop those skills. In reading this book, educators will be encouraged to consider how technology can serve instructional needs in meaningful, authentic ways. Even though technology can be daunting at times, educators will find user-friendly ways to weave new tools seamlessly into instruction.

Perhaps you have never been to, or even heard of, The Forks. Thanks to the 21st century technologies that have changed the way tech-savvy people access information, the chance that you would miss a Jeopardy® question about The Forks is slimmer than ever before. Where some see a digital divide, this book presents an opportunity for educators to jump in. The world is now a global society connected in ways that were only imagined a short time ago. Our students' academic, economic, and personal futures will depend on how we help them understand, navigate, and master the tools and science of their millennium.

How to Use This Book

Can You Hear Me Now?: Applying Brain Research and Technology to Engage Today's Students focuses on bringing educators into the technological loop. This book is designed to get educators thinking about what we are now discovering about learning from multiple perspectives—science, teaching, technology, and educational psychology—and how the findings from experts in these fields can influence student performance. Our role is part translator and part travel guide. Our goal is to make current research accessible and thought-provoking in ways that will encourage further exploration.

Each chapter in this book begins with *Ruminations* which feature our observations of and experiences with the concepts introduced in the chapter. It is our hope that these thoughts resonate with educators, providing a foundation for their engagement in the ideas shared. In this same vein, each chapter ends with *Thinking and Teaching in 2.0*, a feature that provides hands-on tasks related to the content of the chapter. These learning activities enable educators to reflect on the ideas presented in the chapter, and to be able to utilize them with individual colleagues or their professional learning communities. Throughout the chapters, items of general interest or particular relevance are highlighted. We also include descriptions of the digital technologies Lisa has incorporated into her instruction. We hope these examples will serve as models for educators' own practice.

To aid educators in their efforts of becoming better informed about brain research, learning, and digital technologies in the classroom, we have provided resources for further reading as well as links to many of the resources integrated throughout the book. In Appendix A, you will find a list of some of our favorite resources what it means to teach effectively in the 21st century. For your convenience, we have listed all web-based resources mentioned in the body of the book in Appendix B, and all of the references cited in the chapters are listed in Appendix C.

Overviews

The chapters in this book are the following:

- Chapters 1 and 2, *Student 1.0 is Still Alive and Well in Your Classroom* and *The Shift that Matters*, begin the discussion on teaching and learning in the 21st century and the influences that science, technology, and new media have on our students, our teaching, and how society looks at education.

- Chapter 3, *Educator 2.0: Using Cognitive Science to Inform Teaching*, looks at some of the salient points with which neuroscience provides educators and how these can help improve teaching style.

- Chapters 4, 5, and 6, *Professional Learning Relationships in Schools, Connecting Meaningful Learning to the Power of Practice*, and *Tools for Authoring, Collaborating, and Organizing Content and Ideas*, delve into the frameworks that can help support weaving important findings into daily practice in meaningful ways. In short, these chapters illustrate some ways to begin translating research into action.

- Chapter 7, *Social Networking and Online Presence*, takes a hard look at social networking and the influence it has on teaching, learning, and future success.

- Chapter 8, *Technology Is Not an Event*, sows the seeds of change, encouraging educators to bring technology out of the lab and into the classroom.

Each chapter launches readers into a different leg of the same journey that we continue to take. It is our hope that this journey equally informs and inspires further reading, questioning, and experimentation.

Nothing is more frustrating than feeling left out. *Can You Hear Me Now? Applying Brain Research and Technology to Engage Today's Students* attempts to build a bridge between science, research, and classroom practices. We hope it is akin to getting all the right people to a great dinner party, where the discussion pulls the right strings and pushes the right buttons, and, before you know it, everyone realizes they have been sitting at the table together for hours. If you leave this book with a renewed sense of curiosity and inspiration to dig deeper then, in some small way, we have been successful.

Chapter 1

Student 1.0 Is Still Alive and Well in Your Classroom

Ruminations

The shift is subtle at first. You un-tether your phone from the landlines in your house and take it with you wherever you go. Instead of heading to the bookshelf for information, you perform a Google™ search. You do not worry about having a map in your car or even a printout of the directions from an online mapping service because you have a GPS enabled on your phone that reads the directions aloud to you and recalculates them when you go off route. Finally, technology is making life easier, rather than more complicated. Before you know it, you have an e-book reader in your hand, music on your smart phone, and you cannot remember the last time you rented a video or DVD.

Then, the trouble begins. You wait impatiently for your flight to reach cruising altitude so that you can take out your personal electronic devices and start working. You pull up your online version of the newspaper and realize, as you click away on the embedded links in the advice column, that you never finish reading the paper front to back (or back to front) like you used to. You realize this shift again when you are in the car and reach for the rewind button on the radio station, just like you do with your DVR when you watch TV.

Soon, you will fondly remember the good old days when you actually had to type your queries into the search engine on your desktop computer that was hardwired to the Internet, rather than using your hands-free smart phone's voice recognition application.

Too late for nostalgia in that regard. There is already an app for that.

How is our mental acuity faring since we do not have to work as hard to find the information that helps us answer our questions? How is life different today now that technology is serving us better? Perhaps life will not be as different as we think.

Sharing Our School Day with the Digital Natives

Ninety-seven percent of today's teachers have one or more computers in their classrooms; the average ratio of students to computers in these classrooms is 5.3 to 1, with well over ninety percent of those computers connected to the Internet (Gray, Thomas, and Lewis 2010). And, some days it may seem as if the most accessible technical support for those computers is the students who are sitting at the keyboards.

These same students are growing up in a world where they are more likely to buy individual songs instead of albums, where they can download a library book rather than physically check it out, and where they have a virtual network of friends and acquaintances that number in the hundreds (or thousands) and span the globe. Are we prepared for these brave new wired—or perhaps more correctly, wireless—citizens of the world? Does instruction need to be substantially different to ensure that we reach these digital natives of the 21st century?

To be sure, there are those who will try to cajole educators into thinking that the doors of our schools and classrooms are portals to the past (Christensen and Horn 2010; Davidson 2011; Foundation for Excellence in Education 2010; Heffernan 2011; Johnson, Adams, and Haywood 2011). They tell us that thinking nowadays is a whole new beast, and that adults will always be foreigners in the new digital world. They speak of rich new worlds that our students inhabit outside the school walls, a world they must leave behind when they come to learn in school. To these authors, perhaps this otherness seems exotic or provocative. We certainly can draw a digital line in the sand and put all the techies on one side and everyone else on the other, but to do so seems counterproductive. In fact, it is a turn off. It is disconcerting to think that the unceasing movement of time that forces our travel into the future will leave us stranded as strangers in a strange land. In a time when we are gaining unprecedented insights into how human beings learn and have a massive array of tools and resources at our disposal, it is unlikely that we will be marooned.

Chances are you have read an article, seen a report, or been to a workshop where the drumbeat was sounding, broadcasting concerns that schools today are not evolving fast enough to address all these changes in learning or taking advantage of all that technology has to offer learners. Some may even opine that nothing short of a major overhaul of the education system will save our students in time to be prepared for the 21st century. Davidson (2011), for example, observes that 65 percent of today's grade-school students may end up doing work that has not been invented yet. Nonetheless, it is true that educational institutions have changed. Technology has advanced, transforming the way we live, work, play, and learn. Attitudes have shifted. Society has progressed. However, the evolution of a species usually takes longer than a decade—by a magnitude of a thousand or more. The process of thinking has not changed much since *Homo sapiens* first realized that they were doing it (Rotherham and Willingham 2010).

So, even as our students' ability to find and share information via online devices continues to grow in ways we cannot begin to imagine, the same communication skills—both intracranial or intercranial—that were valuable in the past will continue to be so today.

Students need to learn to read—whether they learn from a book on paper or on a screen. They need to learn to write, not just use a keyboard. Research shows that writing by hand trains the brain in ways that keyboarding cannot (Bounds 2010). Students need to be able to observe the conventions of their language so that those reading it can understand it. Reeves (2010) highlights the importance of writing, particularly nonfiction writing, as having "significant and positive effects in nearly every other area of the curriculum. Nonfiction writing is the backbone of a successful literacy and student achievement strategy" (46). In addition, students need to be able to speak intelligibly and listen carefully. They need to be able to organize their thoughts on paper, in a word-processing document, and in their heads.

The great part about today's world is that we have so many new, effective tools to help students read, write, and think! But in using these advanced tools, we will not find ourselves transported to an utterly unknown space and time where thinking is new and different. The tools might be new, but the thinking? It is the same old thinking as before—a difficult, wonderful march from sparse, disconnected chaos, to a rich, ordered network.

Finding Clarity in a Sea of Distraction!

"Immersing myself in a book or a lengthy article used to be easy," Nicholas Carr, a writer and researcher, explains. "My mind would get caught up in the narrative or the turns of the argument, and I'd spend hours strolling through long stretches of prose" (Carr 2008a, 57). Anyone who has taught middle school students, especially those with unlimited text messaging, knows what a permanent state of partial attention looks like. Reading or searching online, for most of us, replicates this state of mind.

It seems as if the Internet has had the effect of maximizing our predisposition for distraction. Links to other articles, ads, related products, and a myriad of keywords with related content are embedded in nearly every page you access. Clicking a link leads you to a new site, which you are likely to scan in seconds to determine whether or not the site is of interest or importance to you. Before too long, you can easily be twenty clicks away from the original article you intended to read and find yourself shopping for Aunt Sally's birthday present.

In a report broadcast on National Public Radio on June 11, 2007, David Weinberger aptly describes a hierarchical diagram of connected facts on the Internet by noting that "the map of links looks like it's been drawn by drunken spiders." He goes on to say, "but that messiness enriches what we know." Information is embedded "in multiple contexts and we get to walk down the paths we find inviting."

Have we unwittingly designed the Internet in our brains' own image? Yes and no. It is true that in both systems, the connected points number in the billions. It is also true that in both systems, there are multiple contexts for accessing and understanding the information that we have. However, the brain appears to be far more organized than the Internet. It is methodically organized, regularly pruned, and becomes more efficient in the areas that are used repeatedly.

Activity involving the brain does not always look organized and efficient. For example, consider the teen who believes she is multitasking as she opens a chat window, her Facebook™ page, an online article about osmosis she is suppose to read for homework, and a blog post she is writing about the concert she is going to over the weekend. If she is a reflective thinker, she often asks herself why it takes her so long to finish her homework. That is an important question, and the answer is telling. In this case, we are observing Student 1.0, the learner who has the same brain structure as a child in ancient times, who has been left high and dry. She does not understand why it takes her so long to do her homework—assuming, of course, that she actually does it!

Her thinking and use of time are not in the least organized or efficient. In the classroom, this same restless student scans the room every five minutes to see what all of her friends and classmates are doing.

Some Thoughts about Multitasking

William Deresiewicz (2010) noted that multitasking impairs your ability to think. He states:

> A study by a team of researchers at Stanford came out a couple of months ago. The investigators wanted to figure out how today's college students were able to multitask so much more efficiently than adults. How do they manage to do it, the researchers asked? The answer, they discovered—and this is by no means what they expected—is that they don't....And here's the really surprising finding: the more people multitask, the worse they are, not just at other mental abilities, but at multitasking itself.

> They [multitaskers] were worse at distinguishing between relevant and irrelevant information and ignoring the latter. In other words, they were more distractible. They were worse at what you might call "mental filing": keeping information in the right conceptual boxes and being able to retrieve it quickly. In other words, their minds were more disorganized. And they were even worse at the very thing that defines multitasking itself: switching between tasks (5).

It is important to remember that the girl in our example has a brain that, in a different place or time, would have saved her village because she was constantly watching the horizon for predators and

26

danger. She is tapping into genes and patterns of attention that served human beings well in both our recent and distant past.

As our imagination fills with images of foraging bands of teenagers crossing the ice and snow, texting one another as they spot saber-toothed tigers amongst the glaciers ("OMG! C@ on ur left!"), it is important to realize that our species survives because of genes. But it is equally important to understand that our species flourishes because of memes. *Meme*, a term coined by Richard Dawkins in his book *The Selfish Gene* (1976), is a transmission device like a gene. "Just as genes propagate themselves in the gene pool by leaping from body to body via sperms or eggs, memes propagate themselves in the meme pool by leaping from brain to brain via a process which, in the broad sense, can be called imitation" (192). Instead of transmitting genetic information, a meme transmits cultural information.

In evolutionary terms, reading and writing are still new. These memes, perhaps the most important inventions of humankind, have helped advance our cultures, the sciences, and understanding at an increasingly accelerated pace throughout our history on this planet. Reading and writing can seem so natural that it is easy to forget we have only been using our brains to become literate for a few thousand years. Some researchers say that it is likely we are recycling neurons previously associated with survival and repurposing them for tasks associated with literacy (Dehaene 2009; Wolf 2007). From survival to culture. From genes to memes; and even newer than memes, temes: what Susan Blackmore calls "technology memes"—the dizzying array of tools with which we now process and present the written word (Blackmore 2008).

Remember the first time students started using word-processing or multimedia presentation programs in the classroom? Were they more focused on font styles, sizes, and how they could animate the pictures and text than on the content of their paper or presentation? However exciting any new tools may be, educators have to be judicious in choosing and applying them—and then teach students how to be judicious in their choice and application of the same tools and techniques. Underneath all of these programs, websites, and mobile applications is a human learner. Educators' focus must be on the students in the classroom and the key content they must learn.

If they are truly dealing with an increasingly distracted student population, then clarity in communication, curriculum, and instruction becomes even more important. If educators are to make abstract concepts more accessible to students, they must carefully select the images, objects, sounds, and actions present to make these concepts more readily understood. If our time becomes increasingly constrained, they must make their choices thoughtful, cogent, concise, and informed by what they know about how students learn and the influence their choices will have on their learning.

Inner Space: The New Frontier

Take a moment and look back on the teachers who not only influenced how you learned, but inspired you to continue learning outside of their classrooms. Think about the teachers you hope your own children will have. What characteristics do they possess? Are they curious? Energetic? How can you tell they still study, read, and learn?

Can you remember the teacher who loved wordplay? Who got worked up about a science experiment? Who read as many new books as he or she assigned to their students? Who loved the patterns and beauty behind solving problems with numbers? Chances are you achieved more in each of these classes; your vocabulary grew, you picked up at least one or two more books, and math seemed challenging, not daunting. Try this experiment: whatever subject you are teaching, ask your students what kind of teacher they most enjoy learning from—someone who loves her subject and shares her passion, or someone who teaches her subject without revealing her passion for it. Who do you think they will pick? Most of us are well aware of our predilections when it comes to subject matter. It is not a coincidence that the units educators love most are likely to be the ones in which their students' performance and engagement is the highest. When students learn, they do not simply learn the content, they also learn whether or not to like or appreciate what they are learning.

As we work our way through the 21st century, educators must add a new topic to their list of beloved subjects—neuroscience. At the end of this century's first decade, there were more than 30,000 books in print that were related to the brain (Goldberg 2010). Even more importantly, this fascination must be shared with students and colleagues with the same enthusiasm as the vocabulary-loving English teacher, the "mad scientist" chemistry teacher, the number puzzle aficionado mathematics teacher, and the kindergarten teacher who finds a new favorite story to share every day.

Neuroscience Moves Out of the Laboratory

Neuroscience is not just for the laboratory anymore. What does a competent educator need to know about the primary engine behind learning in the human brain? How do educators find reliable, intelligible sources of information about how the brain works? How do they translate all the scientifically based research they encounter into classroom practice?

It turns out that teaching is like brain surgery—a deliberate wiring or rewiring of the brain. The brain is complex, multilayered, interconnected, and immensely powerful. It follows to reason that, if educators are to develop their students' intellect, their instruction and curriculum must likewise be complex, multilayered, interconnected, and immensely powerful. To take advantage of the processing power of the 100 billion neurons and 100 trillion connections (Zimmer 2010) in our students' (and our own) brains, it behooves us to develop a working understanding of how our minds access, process, remember, recall, and apply information.

Each part, or lobe, of the brain is responsible for specialized functions. The occipital lobe processes visual information. The temporal lobe processes auditory information, including speech, and stores long-term memories. Sensory integration is handled by the parietal lobe. And the frontal lobe is responsible for the crowning achievements of judgement, problem solving, and planning. Figure 1.1 shows the different areas of the brain.

Fig. 1.1. Parts of the brain

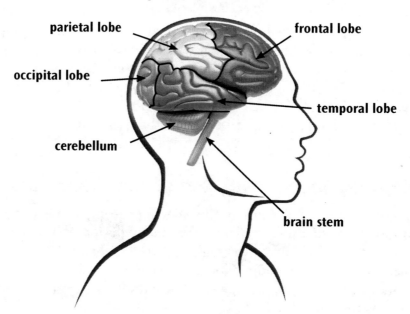

parietal lobe

frontal lobe

occipital lobe

temporal lobe

cerebellum

brain stem

Imagine what it would be like if our instruction could make use of each of these areas to create a more robust understanding of important concepts. Certainly, if you can feel it, experience it, see it, touch it, and hear it, you are more likely to understand and remember and recall it at a later date. Take a moment to reconsider Weinberger's metaphor of the Internet being organized like a web made by drunken spiders (2007). That might be just what our neural network looks like when it lights up and starts recognizing and making sense of facts, figures, and new ideas. Learning and understanding deeply depend on the learner's will to repeatedly focus on the content. This is what builds foundations and develops increasingly efficient neural networks; it always has and always will. Whether a settler is building a sod house on the prairie or an architect is building an undulating skyscraper in a bustling downtown area, there are common foundational elements that must be understood and employed to make each structure stable and habitable.

In later chapters, we will explore the role practice plays in developing expertise in any given area. Being that success in school depends largely on expertise in reading, writing, and developing number sense, educators must first look at how learners make sense of new information and integrate it into the pattern-seeking networks and structures tucked in the folds of their brains.

Appropriately titled, Learning Sciences is emerging as a program of study at more than thirty major universities and research centers around the world, including Northwestern, McGill, Stanford, Tufts, and the University of Sydney. This exciting field combines multiple disciplines (often including cognitive science, computer science, educational psychology, and anthropology) and seeks to uncover what makes for the most effective learning environments. By focusing on real-world settings and taking a multifaceted exploration of how we learn, researchers and students in this field are building exciting bridges between research and practice. Tracey Tokuhama-Espinosa (2011) includes an exhaustive list of these institutions in her book *Mind, Brain, and Education Science: A Comprehensive Guide to the New Brain-Based Teaching*.

Educators can do the same thing in their classrooms and schools by actively engaging themselves in the science of learning, both with and without technology. The following possibilities can be considered: forming a book study group to discuss *Proust and the Squid: The Story and Science of the Reading Brain* (Wolf 2007), getting a subscription to *Scientific American: Mind*, following cognitive psychologist Daniel Willingham's Facebook page, or starting a social bookmarking group to collect and share interesting articles, websites, YouTube™ videos, and more with friends and colleagues. The important thing is simply to share findings, challenge ideas, and look for ways to continually improve how students learn and perform in the classroom.

Shaping Our Future: Outside Forces and How They Influence Education

It used to be that building a computer lab was all that a school or district needed to prepare students for the future. You can almost hear the whisper coming from the computers' cooling fans, "build it, and they will learn." Teachers and administrators struggled with how to integrate technology meaningfully into the curriculum. Should a separate teacher handle technology, because there was not time to squeeze one more thing into the curriculum? In elementary schools, should a computer lab class be added to the art, music, and physical education rotation, so teachers can have more time to meet and plan with grade-level teams?

Slowly but surely, in school board meetings, newspaper columns, and online forums, school communities are grappling with what it means to teach students in the 21st century. To test your own ideas about 21st century skills, imagine that these ideas have been put on trial and you are on the jury. When the prosecuting attorney asks what knowledge you have of 21st century skills, what will your answers be? You might say critical thinking is one of the concepts near the top of your list, although there are those who would disagree. One such example shares a sentiment often echoed by those who follow the movement for greater focus on 21st century skills: "With so much new knowledge being created, content no longer matters; that ways of knowing information are now much more important than information itself" (Rotherham and Willingham 2009, 16). Students believe it when they say, "Why do I have to memorize this? I can always Google it on my smart phone if I need the answer."

Taking advantage of technology to find information rather than learning and recalling facts may be a persuasive argument. That is until your ophthalmologist says, "Huh. Now that's funny. The laser really should not leave a mark like that on your cornea. Hold still a minute. Let me Google that. Oh, don't blink now!"

There are many situations and professions in which one must know the content so well it seems second nature. Such knowledge is crucial to basic competency—let alone expertise. These notions that place ways of knowing information above the information itself will make the 21st century skills movement "a weak intervention for the very students—low-income students and students of color—who need powerful schools as a matter of social equity" (Rotherham and Willingham 2009, 16).

The media and other public voices are constantly questioning the current state of our children's education. It does not take much digging to find expressions of concern that our school systems are hopelessly mired in the past. Pundits and policymakers alike sound clarion calls to draw attention to which partnership, foundation, coalition, or task force needs (or will provide) funding and how their vision will lead to the solutions for our children's future (for examples, see Foundation for Excellence in Education 2010; Johnson, Adams, and Haywood 2011).

Educators cannot avoid addressing the outside forces that are marshaling their arguments for change in the content of the curriculum, the manner in which we instruct, or the tools we share with students. By focusing on a series of critical questions, educators can avoid being led astray from their primary mission—providing a sound education for all their students. Questions such as the following enable educators to move forward with change that benefits teaching and learning:

- How do we know this particular innovation, tool, or resource is important?
- How do we explain why it is important to students, colleagues, and the community?
- How do we convince and teach others that it is important?
- How do we help others implement the change?

In the end, what matters most is how these questions are asked and addressed in each classroom. As educators move forward with new technological tools that are more meaningfully integrated into the curriculum, they must be thoughtful and patient in equal measure. As any teacher will tell you, there is an inverse relationship between our confidence in any tool and how many times it crashes when put to use. It is days like those when we are ready to open the pod bay door and shove HAL right out, plummeting him back to Earth.

Time is a finite and overtaxed resource in any school, especially when it comes to providing classroom teachers with the resources and opportunities to deepen their understanding of how and why we all learn. Between determining how to address grade-level standards, making sense of the data collected from student assessments, designing differentiated learning activities, and preparing sub-plans, the times to process and share scientific research on learning and cognitive development might seem few and far between. Working with tools and media that seem to change between lesson planning and delivery in the classroom can make even the most confident teachers feel wobbly and uncertain.

Challenges in education are always present. Finding and refining the best ways to help young minds grow is hard work. Now, rather than making sure new copies of a classroom novel are the same edition so the pagination on our handouts from the ditto machine do not have to change, we make backup plans for when our interactive whiteboard ignores our attempts to interact with it.

The full potential of education is expressed through the interaction between our experiences and our openness to new ideas and understandings. The argument will never be whether or not to use the new media, technology, and information now at our disposal, but how to use it to better develop understanding and intellect, in both literacy and numeracy. While it is clear that technology (at least until the next operating system is released) is here to stay, educators must continue to remember that their brains have been here all along.

Thinking and Teaching in 2.0: Point/Counterpoint

Consider the difference between a trend and something that is trendy. Headlines, online and in print, often make texting, social networking, and other new media alternately frivolous window dressing to our students' lives or dangerous distractions that will lead to lower standards for literacy and numeracy development. Sit with a colleague and, in point/counterpoint style, use the two stems below to explore your views on 21st century learning tools in school. After your first round, switch sides and make your new arguments based on the opposing stem.

- Technology and new media open these doors to learning...
- Technology and new media create these barriers to learning...

As a result of this conversation or activity, work with colleagues to identify how our perspectives on technology influence our ability to integrate technology into instruction in meaningful ways.

The Shift That Matters

Ruminations

"Just give me an answer I can use."

We have all been there. When the pressure is mounting to get something done, the last thing we want to do is research options, experiment, and reflect on the effectiveness of our choices. Whether it is a beleaguered Midwestern United States community finding a way to free itself from the grips of a blizzard, or peaceful Egyptian citizens in Tahrir Square pushing for access to the global stage, urgency often becomes the most salient feature to finding a solution. Both these stories led the evening news and provided banner headlines online for the better part of a month, as 2011 was still new. Both featured weary citizens who wanted their ordeals to end favorably, quickly, and without a plague of doubts.

Dealing with Change

Chances are you have bought a book, attended a workshop, taken a course, or viewed a webinar hoping for guidance on a myriad of issues teachers face every day: response to intervention, differentiation, closing the achievement gap, or using data to inform instruction. As educators, our success is built upon our students' success, so any direction that helps us fulfill that mission is welcome. Most likely, your school or district has tackled one or more of these issues as an initiative school improvement plan.

Successfully implementing a new initiative is stressful, even when done with the best resources and intentions. Add the pressure of a timeline, test scores that are not increasing at an acceptable rate, budget cuts that undermine teacher morale and threaten to severely limit needed resources, and subgroups of your school population that are not progressing at the rate of your general population—and what you have is a race to anywhere but the top. Exasperation can grasp even the best of teachers, making them feel as if they are student teaching again. "Just tell me what to do," they exclaim. "Then I can start figuring out how to do it well!"

Our goal in this book is to provide educators with answers they can use—ones we hope they can use without becoming exasperated. But first, it is important to reflect on how we can change, what needs to change, and what makes change so difficult.

State and federal policy, scientific and education research, law, society, and the media all have significant influence on trends in education. On some issues, these forces are at odds with one another, while a confluence of ideas is evident about others. Currently, one such area of agreement centers on the idea that good instruction should focus on teaching students rather than teaching content.

School rooms in many commercials, books, plays, television shows, and movies often still show teachers presenting information to students in a technically proficient and professional manner, implying that it is enough for the teacher to stand at the front of the room and make sense. Teaching, in these imagined classes, consists of the teacher simply explaining everything to the students by talking at them. And learning consists of the majority of students quickly understanding what the teacher says. The students who do not get it are always funny or tragic characters, the implication being that there is something wrong with them, not with the instruction, the milieu, or the curriculum.

Now the prevailing theme is more in line with an adage often associated with John Wooden: You haven't taught until they have learned (Nater and Gallimore 2006). Embracing this sentiment would be easier if most social commentary was largely in support of educators. It can be difficult for teachers to find themselves embraced in the current climate of accusation and blame, so often characterized by inaccurate statements about what happens in schools. In order for teachers and principals to be better able to embrace Wooden's adage, they should feel comfortable trying new techniques, making mistakes, and being guided by their professional learning network without feeling the constant risk of a potential pay cut or being dismissed. But sometimes, the measuring tool feels more like a hickory switch than a meter stick.

However we manage to improve, change begins with each and every one of us. Even with an open mind, understanding that improving education is just as much about changing adult behavior as it is changing student behavior might, for some, be a journey out of our comfort zones. To shift to this mindset, everyone involved with education has to accept and consistently communicate that improving educational practice does not imply educators were previously doing poorly. The best way to teach our students to be lifelong learners is to be lifelong learners ourselves.

So, as educators explore what influence neuroscience and new media has on student motivation and learning, here is an essential question to ponder: Is your primary focus on who you are teaching or what you are teaching? This question is crucial because, if educators are truly to embrace the idea that teaching students takes precedence over teaching content, they must also embrace the idea that all students can learn and succeed. Easy to say, but hard to do.

Universal Education Equals Universal Benefits

Throughout our careers, we have worked with families and students from a range of abilities and socioeconomic backgrounds. As do most American teachers, we come from a solidly middle-class upbringing and outlook on life. After two decades in education and education-related fields, we have listened to colleagues and community members at school and social functions alike discuss current trends, pendulum swings, and curriculum mandates. Clearly, we face (and will continue to face) many challenges in our schools, the foremost being equitable access to quality education for all students.

Many recent initiatives seek to address inequity by making sure students of color, students who live in poverty, students with learning disabilities, students with behavior issues, and English language learners do not end up in "silos" where they remain once they are labeled and tracked, never returning to a rich, full general education experience. Effective teachers must have expertise in making data-based instructional decisions and determining specific interventions for students who otherwise could not access content or curriculum, as well as differentiating instruction for students with different learning styles and abilities. In the hands of an expert teacher, these are all good things.

More specifically, these are factors that make us look more critically at how our practice influences our students' potential. They are good things that take an unprecedented amount of time, effort, and expertise for the approximately 3.7 million teachers in elementary and secondary public schools, as well as their administrators, to employ effectively (IES National Center for Education Statistics 2010).

Many of these recent well-intentioned pressures for change in education hold classroom teachers, building principals, and central administrators completely responsible for student progress, even though the many variables involved in the success of any child's education are never completely in their control.

While many initiatives for change are based on sound education research conducted in concert with current classroom practices, many others continue to come from non-educators lacking the very evidence for success they demand from educators.

And, just when the initiatives and mandates educators are tackling with their grade-level and content-area teammates begin to make sense, KJ walks into school and they realize that no matter how well-designed the initiatives are, they alone will never be the great equalizers that we need. KJ is a bright, cheerful, and rambunctious kindergartner with energy to spare. He also drinks a lot of water, especially right when he gets to school. It takes a few days to figure out why.

He is hungry and water takes the edge off. He also sits next to a student who comes to school every day with a thermos full of warm pot stickers—his favorite lunch—of which one or two always end up on the floor. Here's the rub: although these two students might have similar abilities, potential, and parents who are willing to support their children in every way they can, they also come to school with a different range of life experiences.

Hart and Risley's notable research spotlights the disparity in vocabulary development between children from impoverished, working class, and professional families: an estimated thirty million word difference in terms of exposure to spoken words by the time the children in the study were three. A rich working vocabulary, or lack of it, significantly contributes to academic performance, affecting every part of the school day (Hart and Risley 2003).

Before children have one single school experience, their experiences at home and in the community contribute to significant variations in their preparedness for the culture of school. Perhaps the next report on academic inequality between the haves and have-nots will reflect technology and digital literacies in addition to issues of more traditional literacies. Again, in our search for solutions, urgency is front and center. In many ways, we cannot wait to change.

Change Is Different than We Think

We are convinced that mindful and meaningful improvement in education necessitates a thoughtful look at how change is addressed in schools. Federal and state legislation may guide the way we organize our schools, but the choices we make in our classrooms have a profound influence on how well our students learn. From slate to paper, slide rule to calculator, or book to e-reader, there will always be innovations that influence classroom instruction. The key is in how we determine whether or not the innovation is an improvement.

"Change is the new constant," proclaim the editors in their introduction to the 2010 Phi Delta Kappa/*Gallup Poll of the Public's Attitude Towards the Public Schools.* "Yet while we thrive on technological advances, we worry that our social systems can't keep pace with the accelerating rate of change...We can't imagine living without iPods®, Internet, and cell phones, yet we still reminisce about the good old days" (Bushaw and Lopez 2010, 9).

While we may miss our independent record shops and bookstores, it is not likely we will miss the local franchise for renting videos. Why? Could it hinge on the presence and passion of the person behind the counter? Your visit to a clean, well-lit place for books or high fidelity shop was about connecting with someone with similar interests and finding the elusive treasure in the bin, not hoping that of the two dozen copies of the latest new release, only one copy was left.

Working with innovative ideas and regulations aimed at improving education likewise deal with connecting with the right people to find elusive treasures: those tools and techniques that engage students in their learning and education. Even with this as our goal in schools, the task is often daunting.

What Innovation Involves

Let's consider the following scenario to help frame what educators face as they try to improve the service they provide. Imagine an entrepreneur bringing a new concept to market, an idea that will revolutionize how we work and communicate. This concept will make information much more readily available to many more people, promote equity in access to important ideas, and help humankind grow and flourish. The initial market research indicates huge potential for both the public and private sectors. The entrepreneur's challenge is to engage the skeptics. This revolutionary idea is too radical, and professionals in the field are skeptical.

Our history is filled with resistance to successful ideas. As you reflect on the scenario shared in the scenario above, consider the following questions and how they were initially answered:

- Why would anyone pay for overnight delivery? Mail arrives quickly enough at a fraction of the cost.
- Why do I need a mobile phone? If someone needs to get a hold of me, they can just wait until I get home. Alternately, why do a need a phone at home? The only phone I answer is my cell.
- Why would anyone pay to send a typed message over a cell phone? If I want somebody to know something, I can just call them.

- Who needs a computer to send a message to the office next door? If I want to ask somebody a question, I can just walk over and ask or pick up the phone and call.

So what is the name of this revolutionary new medium you want to bring to market?: Writing. Wolf (2007) chronicles Socrates' worries that writing would divert the true meaning of understanding and make students lazy and less able, as they would no longer have to memorize important works. His belief in the oral tradition was certain; it had served civilization well until his point in history. Did Socrates have the mindset or framework to truly understand how writing would set human civilization on a course of exponential expansion? Could he know that eventually, this invention would be one of the primary forces behind transforming civilization from an agrarian to an industrial base?

Although the effort required to overcome resistance to change often results in a better idea, an inability to accept new paradigms that challenge or change how we have always done business often leaves us stuck (and maybe feeling a bit paranoid). This resistance is not simply technophobia, even when you joke about not being able to program your VCR, much less use the extra features of your district's email program. Even as teachers learn more and more about how the brain takes in, retains, and applies new learning, they still are more likely to feel comfortable with how they learned in the classroom when they were children or how they initially learned to teach.

For a visual version of our seemingly natural resistance to change, just do a quick search for "Medieval Helpdesk" on YouTube™. Nearly three million hits later, the original Norwegian version is still the funniest.

It is important to explore how we change or resist change. The question is not "Should we change?" but "How will we change?" The former implies a yes or no; the latter invites degrees of response. This is the paradigm in which we all now teach. Whether we are working with educators or students, parents or policy, change is coming and will continue to come. It is up to us to have a role in defining this change so it helps our students meet their futures with confidence and gives them a hand in their own success.

Giving Students Voice and Responsibility in Learning

Classroom teachers need not take for granted that behavior management, learning, assessing, enforcing rules, accountability, pacing, and homework are solely their responsibility. It is important to share some of that responsibility with students and, in doing so, share some of the power in the classroom (Lent 2010). Think about a critical part of any classroom's literacy block—independent reading. When teachers give the homework assignment for students to read 20 minutes each day, students typically fall into three groups in regards to its completion. Two groups of students are most likely to do the reading: the ones who would have read anyway and the ones who do it because the teacher assigned it. The third group is comprised of the kids who do not read. They have failed to follow directions. The kids who do read are following directions. However, none of that is about reading, which is ostensibly what that assignment is for.

Only one group of students benefits from this assignment, and that benefit comes at a cost. They are the ones who still enjoy the school edition of the game Simon Says: Simon says touch your nose. Simon says jump. Simon says do your homework. Simon Says is a game in which the person with the role of Simon tells the rest of the players what to do. For the players, the fun of the game is in being attentive enough to the cue "Simon says," and competent enough to do what Simon says. A lot of the fun is also in doing the actions dictated by Simon. But the players do not invest any meaning in the actions—clap your hands, blink your eyes, turn around—in and of themselves. The players do not give any thought to whether they would prefer touching an ear to jumping, or which of those actions would be best for their physical health or hand-eye coordination. The idea that kids would be concerned with the beneficial qualities of playing Simon Says is ridiculous.

The worry is that classroom life is sometimes too much like Simon Says. Instead it is "Teacher Says," and the fun, for some students, is in being attentive enough to teacher cues and competent enough to do what the teacher says. Perhaps some of the actions—answering textbook questions, finishing worksheets, organizing papers—are fun for some kids. But what if, like in Simon Says, the students do not invest any meaning in the actions? If we are indeed developing lifelong learners, we want students to be reflective about the beneficial qualities of the learning activities they are doing.

The Simon Says kids will do the reading because the teacher assigned it. They are willing and able to comply, but it is like ordering a kid to apologize. No one can ever know if it is genuine because the kid was ordered to do it. Even the kid issuing the mandated apology is probably unsure of its meaning. If the only reason a student is reading is because her teacher told her to, then what would she answer if she were asked to set a purpose for reading? Given what we know about authentic purpose being crucial to reading comprehension, how well would she comprehend what she read with "My teacher told me to," as a purpose?

It is obvious that this is a negative situation for the students who failed to do their homework. Surprisingly though, this situation is also negative for the students who would have read regardless of whether it was assigned or not. What is the message they get when they are told to do what they would have done anyway? It is the way you feel when you see a loved one, arms full of packages, who needs a door opened. And just as you register that, the person says, "Uh, a little help here?" You sputter, "I was going to! Just give me a second!" It's insulting. You think, "What kind of person do you think I am? Don't you trust me?"

Whenever we are in a situation in which we want someone else to do something, we have to recognize that the individual must show some willingness or desire to do what we request.

No one can make a student behave or do his homework without the student's cooperation or coercion of some kind. Even with coercion, a teacher cannot make a child want to learn, or understand a concept. That desire has to originate inside the learner.

Two-way trust is crucial to a productive teacher-student relationship. Teachers have to trust that students want to learn—want to open that door before being asked. Teachers must believe that if the student is not doing so, there is a good reason and the reason is worth finding. Occasionally, we need to give students the silence of their own minds, without our input, and trust that they can be reflective and self-critical. And students need to feel safe in order to risk trying something difficult and sometimes failing. They will be reluctant to engage in such behaviors if the teacher or other students are harsh critics. Accepting this is not so much a teaching style, but a reality to embrace. We will describe this reality further in Chapter 5.

Silence Is Golden

Faced with the drastic unevenness of student background knowledge, most teachers feel the urgent need to fix it. Many of us mistakenly believe we can fix misconceptions and lack of background knowledge for students by explaining everything to everyone. It is exhausting and largely fruitless. No one can fix someone else's "broken" concept or patch holes in the background knowledge. Students need to do that themselves. Teachers should create an environment in which students can build their own concepts about new ideas, as well as recognize and fix their own misconceptions.

Having a clear philosophy of teaching helps classroom teachers make the countless real-time decisions they are faced with each day. A part of that philosophy should be guidelines about when to speak and when to stay quiet—a philosophy of exposition. Teachers should talk when they are:

- having a conversation with a student or a group of students.
- reading aloud to them.
- sharing part of their life (e.g., telling students a little about their family or garden). This should be limited in depth and duration as should the rest of the items.
- giving directions, setting limits, explaining classroom routines and scheduling.
- asking high quality questions. (But, students learn more effectively when they are asking the questions, so a teacher's question should be carefully chosen.)
- answering a question that a student posed if the answer is relevant, and the asker or another student cannot answer it.
- modeling good thinking. There should be a time limit on this depending on grade level and the concept being modeled.

Otherwise, students should be talking, as we learn best when we are active, not passive.

When Change Is at Your Door

As we face the change that comes to our classrooms and schools, no magical silver bullet appears to solve the challenges that teachers encounter. Complex issues deserve thoughtfulness and willingness to work hard at finding solutions. Teachers need information, time, and strategies to adequately address the opinions and pressures that come from society, media, and policy-makers. Providing such accommodations is more than professional respect; it gives teachers a modicum of control over policies and practices that are being put into place in each school and district. And sometimes, that is enough.

The following are a few strategies and ideas that can help teachers and administrators navigate change and the pressures it can bring to a school or district:

- Be aware of the climate and concerns with education in your community, state, and nation. During the economic collapse in 2009, we lost our confidence in those who were charged with watching and protecting our investments simply because they seemed incredibly unaware of what was happening and unable to mitigate the damages. No one likes an unpleasant surprise and nothing inspires confidence like the well-timed sharing of well-founded knowledge.

- Be proud to be a coach and facilitator in your classroom. The original meaning of the word *coach* is a vehicle that conveyed a willing rider from one place to a chosen destination. When we see ourselves as coaches who develop expertise, it allows us to have a growth mindset in regards to our students, and gives us a clear framework for integrating good ideas into our classrooms (e.g., How will this new action or resource help my students to better access and understand this important content, and how will it help them grow?)

- Take stock of your instruction in terms of inspiration and aspiration. Our goal as educators is to inspire our students' learning or to help them aspire to improve. Inspiration speaks to the sense of wonder crucial to helping curious minds develop; aspiration speaks to the value of the hard work it takes to improve at important tasks. How do the tools and ideas we use to instruct and assess our students help them better access learning?

- Take the role of being a learning leader seriously. While coaches may help students get to where they want to be, a leader takes students to places they did not know they wanted to be. Just as school leaders must share and build their vision with their staff, teachers must build a shared vision for successful learning with their students. We all learn best when we believe in what we are doing.

No matter how exciting and entrancing the tools of this millennium turn out to be, we still need to make sure our practices help us reach all students. We do not want to look at neuroscience, new media, technology tools, and browser-based reading and interaction as simple icing or window dressing for the classroom. There is simply too much at stake to "gadget-ize" the tools and resources that are in place in each classroom today. Students need to be able to make informed, examined decisions about the content they learn, the tools they use to access that learning, and the ways in which they communicate understanding.

It probably is no surprise that both the architecture of the brain and of school systems changes slowly. So why does it feel like change always comes at a breakneck pace? Why does it feel as if the next great thing has to be implemented now and with fidelity, or else all that you hold to be true is plummeting into the abyss? One piece of advice we can give is to take a deep breath and picture Chevy Chase in his Saturday Night Live shark suit knocking at your door. With a little humor and perseverance, you are ready to maintain with integrity the important practices you and your colleagues can demonstrate to be effective for all students.

Thinking and Teaching in 2.0: Taking Stock before Taking First Steps

Wait for it. Wait for it. Few things unnerve a new teacher quite like the empty gaze and silence following an unanswered question, especially during an observation by an administrator. One of our favorite moments was watching a colleague have such a moment. You could hear a pin drop as she turned, walked to the board, and wrote, "The average teacher waits seven seconds for students to respond. I am not average." A few moments later, students took over with smiles and much to contribute. For a variety of reasons, making the shift to take advantage of the advances in neuroscience, technology, and new media may be uncomfortable at the outset. Any journey begins first with the question, "Why am I doing this?" Take stock of what encourages you and what daunts you, and use those ideas to set some achievable goals. Consider:

- Changing or updating aspects of my pedagogy in light of new insights in neuroscience and new tools for 21st century learning is exciting because...
- Changing or updating aspects of my pedagogy in light of new insights in neuroscience and new tools for 21st century learning is daunting due to...

Make a list of personal learning goals based on your responses to this activity. Rank these goals in order from least important to most important.

Next, do a second ranking from least realistic to most realistic:

- What decisions will you make in light of your ordering of the goals in terms of importance and realistic chance of success?
- In what ways did the combination of importance and realistic chance of success influence your decisions?

Consider the following quote:

"We are called to be the architects of the future, not its victims."

—R. Buckminster Fuller (n.d.)

- What do you think the implications of this quotation are for you and your colleagues?

Chapter 3

Educator 2.0: Using Cognitive Science to Inform Teaching

Ruminations

While packing his office in preparation for a recent school construction project, Jerry reluctantly boxed his inherited treasure trove of curriculum binders spanning the last decade of curriculum updates. Sorely tempted to use the same method employed for clearing out old journals and projects at home (put it in a box in the basement and, after a year, if the box is still closed, throw it out), he nonetheless returned them to his bookcase once the construction was complete.

It used to be that curriculum updates and new initiatives were delivered in a brand new three-ring binder. If that binder was lucky, it made it to a visible bookshelf to gather dust; if not, it ended up in a filing cabinet or closet. As we transition from the three-ring binder era to online collections of related, editable documents, it is important for educators to remain focused on student learning. Is the binder, electronic or virtual, accessed regularly enough that a page, bookmark, or file can be found with ease? Are the curriculum resources organized in such a way that it can easily capitalize on the power and efficacy of these new tools to enhance student learning? At all costs, we do not want to go the way of the curriculum binder by either gathering dust after a single use. Given the myriad of educational fads that come and go, teachers need a guide that can help them make instructional decisions that are effective and enduring. Cognitive science—a nexus between neuroscience, computer science, psychology, philosophy, and anthropology—can be a steadying force in educational decision-making.

Ubiquitous social sites, new media, masses of information, and access to global society have changed the way tech-savvy people obtain and interact with information. In some cases, less-than tech-savvy people are affected, too. Have you "friended" your parents yet? Have you "unfriended" anyone? Has anyone "unfriended" you?

Technology also provides students more choices about how to show what they know. Podcasts, multimedia presentations, and wikis are increasingly familiar ways for students to produce and consume information (Bean 2010). Their expertise in using technology can be unsettling, as students will often have greater comfort plugging in than their teachers.

Texting, social networking, Google, and the thousands of other tools at our students' disposal may change how they are able to access and utilize information. But, do these resources change how students learn? In the midst of these surface changes, cognitive science reveals that the brains of today's students are "wired" in very much the same way as those of students in the past. Our focus in this chapter will be on how educators can use the tenets of cognitive science to effectively deliver instruction that maximizes students' ability to grow academically and emotionally. Although the ideas presented here are grounded in cognitive science, they are by no means comprehensive.

Building a Bridge between Research and Practice

The need for ongoing professional development is a consequence of the many recent changes in schools including, for example, response to intervention, standards-based report cards, data-informed decision-making, and media literacy. In fact, it is not hard to imagine, in a conference room deep in the belly of a state department of education, a conversation such as this:

> State Official #1: Ben, how many requirements do we have left to check off on our federal application for additional funding?

> State Official #2: Um, Tess, I only have the forms here for unfunded mandates from the federal government, the ones labeled, "Efficiency and Accountability Forms 1-10."

> State Official #3: Same thing, I think. We started work on items one through twelve two years ago, but then the funding ran out because we weren't in an election cycle.

> State Official #1: Well, we have to solve these issues now, using scientifically based methods and materials.

> State Official #2: I'll see what publisher has those materials. How will we get our teachers ready for these changes?

> All (with feeling): Professional Development!

> State Official #3: Great, I see there is funding here for that! Now, who do we go to for professional development?

> Silence settles over the conference table.

We all have sat through professional development sessions that were not as beneficial as we had hoped and left us feeling frustrated. Perhaps this is a reason why teachers can often be such a challenging audience to teach. Satire aside, there is a reason why we raise the specter of questionable professional development and research. As we review cognitive science—and especially brain research—we must guard against oversimplification and ideas that are generalized too quickly.

Many experts and many intriguing findings are available to review, but if you come across any definitive statements about the relationship between brain research and pedagogy, take caution. Myths about neuroscience and the application of its findings for the classroom abound, with some information at best misleading and, at worst, dead wrong (Willis 2007; 2008). Nonetheless, cognitive scientist Daniel T. Willingham (2009) acknowledges: "The mind is at last yielding its secrets to persistent scientific investigation. We have learned more about how the mind works in the last twenty-five years than we did in the previous twenty-five hundred" (1). Small and Vorgan (2008) write about the influence of technology on the development of the brain and note that today's young people, dubbed "Digital Natives," are the most sensitive to this influence. They state: "Daily exposure to high technology—computers, smart phones, video games, search engines like Google and Yahoo™— stimulates brain cell alternation and neurotransmitter release, gradually strengthening new neural pathways in our brains while weakening old ones (1).

The flood of findings in brain science is exciting. As educators, we would be remiss if we did not explore these ideas and try to apply them to instruction. The question is how to get the clear and meaningful information so educators can begin to affect change where it matters the most—in the classroom. Consider the following recommendations:

- Do your own exploring of the topics with a healthy dose of skepticism. If a claim is not supported, reject it, accept it with reservation, or search out other authorities who verify or dispute the claim.

- Do not fall head-over-heels in love with an idea until there is acceptable evidence that it is true.

- Be ready to revise what you thought you knew. The lists of resources in Appendix A and references in Appendix C will help you in your quest for credible information.

While findings from cognitive science offer powerful tools for instruction, collaboration can supercharge it! If educators are trying something new in their classroom or school, they will be able to clearly judge its efficacy if their colleagues or teammates try it, too. And if they find something that works, their collaboration ensures their solution has a wider audience than their classroom.

Big Ideas from Cognitive Science

The new millennium has ushered in a cavalcade of titles from notable scientists, researchers, and writers exploring the advances made in brain research. Much of the work that we reference in this book is just as likely to be found on the shelves of your neighborhood bookstore as it is in a reference library. Scientists, writers, psychologists, and researchers are learning to ask questions and make observations ranging from how we learn to read to how we are motivated to learn, as well as the impact of technology on our brains and fundamental social skills. These individuals have uncovered fascinating details about the inner workings of our minds and motivation that can profoundly influence a new era of education.

The physical and philosophical underpinnings of schools have always reflected the priorities of the age in which they exist. From the austerity of early schools in an agrarian economy, a shift to an assembly-line mentality in the industrial age took place. As we shifted to the information age and computers became commonplace in schools, schools became more responsive to students' individual needs and, paradoxically, sought out common standards for all students.

Number crunching as the exclusive domain of computers, complex tax code handled by software, and computer programming jobs shipped overseas indicate a shift away from American society's value for linear thinking. As Daniel Pink writes, "The keys to the kingdom are changing hands." As we move to what he calls the Conceptual Age, our economy and society are "built on inventive, empathic, big-picture capabilities" (Pink 2006, 1). People who have expertise in areas that are impossible for computers to handle are poised to be powerful in today's world.

In these times, people do not just expect the Internet to make all the information known to humankind accessible to them. They expect to be creators of that information as well. They do not expect to be held hostage by incomprehensible technological tools. They expect to be the tools' masters. Teachers have an important role in helping students become masters of technology rather than slaves to it. Our understanding of the more significant recent findings from cognitive science and the potential influence of these on curriculum, instruction, and classroom management will enable us to do just that. At the same time, we will expand our own level of skill and confidence to meet the challenges of the fast pace of technological change.

Why Educators Must Embrace the Potential of Plasticity

In *The Brain that Changes Itself: Stories of Personal Triumph from the Frontiers of Brain Science*, Norman Doidge (2007) shares captivating stories that help us understand an important paradigm shift. For hundreds of years, everyone knew that once childhood was over, the brain was unchanging until the decline associated with old age. It was accepted that you were defined by the brain cells you were born with, which also mapped out your potential capacity for learning. All brain damage was permanent. You had nowhere to go but down.

This thinking began to unravel in the 1960s and 70s with clear evidence of the human brain's ability to change, shift resources, and heal. The idea of neuroplasticity has become a popular one because it holds out hope for healing and for progress. The flip side is that we might be more vulnerable to unwanted outside influences than we thought (Doidge 2007).

As of this writing, the term *neuroplasticity* is the recipient of some criticism. It seems, to some, such a general term as to be rendered meaningless. But for teachers, who might not be neuroscientists but are just as concerned about brains as they are, the concept of brain plasticity can be a useful way of considering students' learning.

Why Educators Must Understand that Talent Takes Work

How does a student make progress? What makes a student gifted? Why do the complicated maneuvers of an athlete or a musician seem second nature and automatic? Most importantly, is ability the privilege of only a chosen few or can educators harness the power of meaningful, purposeful practice in our everyday classroom instruction? In *The Talent Code: Greatness Isn't Born. It's Grown. Here's How.*, Daniel Coyle (2009) reassures us that regardless of how innate talent looks, greatness is not something we are born with. It is something that we grow. He demonstrates that students will learn as long as they engage in deep practice and have a teacher or coach who knows how to spark motivation. He does not pretend that these ingredients are easy to come by, but he does describe how to create them.

A Classroom Anecdote: The Power of Purposeful Effort

After reading Coyle's book, Lisa was somewhat skeptical until the day she read *How Much Is a Million* (Schwartz 1985) to her fifth graders. In this book, the author's analogies and the illustrator's drawings brilliantly make the concept of a million accessible to elementary school students. They show how long it would take to count to one hundred, to one thousand, and then to one million. Amidst the gasps and wows in class as Lisa read,

Mitchell put up his hand. He proclaimed, "Yeah, I once counted to a million but it wasn't all at once and I did it a little each day and I had to remember where I left off but it took me about 3 months." And then all was quiet in room 240.

"What on Earth could make a person want to spend his time that way?" is an excellent question that addresses motivation. It is important to note that Mitchell attended a math class at the middle school each day so that he could be admitted to the honors math class two grade levels above his own. He did not come out of the womb two years ahead in math. Of his own volition, Mitchell engaged in focused, purposeful thought about mathematics because it was not just about counting to a million. There were countless other times that math was on Mitchell's mind. Coyle explains to his readers how a student gets to be so motivated to learn and how teachers can use that formula to inspire other students who lack motivation.

Why Educators Must Believe that All Students Can Succeed

Early in Jerry's teaching career, a colleague shared a piece of advice about spelling tests and fifth-graders. "When you give back that first spelling test," she advised, "Don't praise Alex or Susan for their perfect test by exclaiming how they must have done such a great job studying. Chances are they didn't study at all for that first test. Once you've praised them for effort they didn't give, they are not likely to study for harder spelling tests that come down the road."

Great advice, and certainly it has broader application than spelling tests for fifth-graders. How we talk to students matters, not simply for their esteem, but for their achievement. So how do we give students meaningful feedback and encouragement that engenders ongoing and purposeful effort?

Carol Dweck (2006) captures this conundrum quite succinctly with a provocative question: "If you have the ability, why should you need learning?" (24). She and her colleagues set out to explore this question with an equally provocative experimental design by conducting studies with hundreds of students, mostly early adolescents. Given a slightly challenging task to complete ten questions from a nonverbal IQ test, students were alternately praised for their ability or their effort after successfully completing the task.

Although equal to begin with, the praised-for-ability and praised-for-effort groups quickly began to separate on subsequent tasks. Those who were beginning to attribute their success to natural ability were less willing to take on new challenges; those who were beginning to attribute their success to effort were more willing to take on new challenges. The latter group seemed to gain a resiliency that those in the other group did not possess. And when presented with challenges of equal difficulty later on, the latter group actually performed better.

When students and teachers look at ability as a fixed, immutable gift, they begin building barriers that could take a lifetime to tear down. Here is the choice many students face: Do I try to do something that I know is hard and could lead to my making mistakes and looking unintelligent? Or do I only attempt what I know I can be successful at with minimal effort so I can always appear in control and competent?

Our media-driven culture places a high value on effortless ability. As a result, society unwittingly conveys the message: If you have to work at it, you must not be any good at it. Such messages severely undermine children's ability to learn, as well as our own ability to learn and teach.

Strategies that Matter

Even though cognitive science gives us promising directions, all it takes is one look at state standards, your current district initiatives, and your school's curriculum to recognize time is at a premium in the 21st century classroom. Good ideas, without implementation, are either forgotten or a source of frustration. Couple time demands with the pressures of accountability, and teachers may feel even less flexible in their day-to-day and moment-to-moment decision-making than ever before.

So what is an educator to do? Let's review some of the recent insights we have gained from cognitive science:

- **Plasticity**—The brain has unknown potential for growth and is not limited by a predetermined natural ability.
- **Meaningful practice**—Learning is greatly enhanced by engaging in focused practice that is in the learner's control. Effort, engagement, and ability to assess and correct mistakes along the way all have significant influence on developing expertise.
- **Expectations aid motivation**—When teachers promote the importance of effort over ability, both explicitly and implicitly, all students do better.

Any one of these points is easily defensible as a solid philosophy for designing classroom instruction. How often have we read a great book or article, attended an invigorating conference, or been inspired by a conversation with colleagues, only to return to our classrooms unable to answer the question, "Now what?"

Plasticity in the Classroom

Exciting new ideas deserve sharing. As we devoured books by Doidge (2007), Wolf (2007), and other cognitive scientists, we shared our ideas with everyone. It is hard not to, as neuroscience helps all of us understand our inner space and grow in confidence and ability. However, inevitably, whether at a dinner party or team meeting, doubts eventually would begin to arise about how much influence we have over our own expertise. The first opposition usually comes from the field of athletics in the form of a statement: "Sure, you want to be a player in the NBA. But if you are only five and a half feet tall, it really doesn't matter what you want." That may be true enough, but it all depends on how you define expertise. (By the way, Spud Webb won the 1986 NBA All-Stars Slam Dunk contest in Dallas, Texas. He was five foot six.)

The more troubling opposition comes from those who cling to the idea of innate ability and its relationship to student success. Some of those conversations are downright depressing. When we shared some of the more prominent evidence with an educator associated with a Midwest state's organization for gifted children, he dismissed the entire concept of plasticity and student potential with one statement: "You can't make a silk purse out of a sow's ear."

Casting aside concerns for any educator with such a bleak opinion of students who do not meet standards, consider this: What is it like for students who show up at school every day thinking that the keys to the academic kingdom are not something within their grasp? Once children, or adults for that matter, identify their ability to learn as out of their control, serious roadblocks to academic—and eventually economic—success are in place.

We all have anecdotes from friends, colleagues, and our own lives which bemoan personal ability in mathematics, writing, or another area. ("Ask me to do anything more than balance my checkbook, and I am lost!" or "Thank goodness for spell-check.") Imagine if students had that same kind of attitude about their learning. "Not much imagination is needed," you might be saying to yourself. "Those students are in my classroom every year."

The brain's plasticity is a true promise for maximizing the potential of every student. The ability students bring to school is their starting point, not their finish line. It is our job to help children and their families understand that. Ways to achieve this could include the following:

- Share information about brain research. In an authentic and engaging manner, explain findings from neuroscience to help students and their families understand the importance of effort. At open houses and parent conferences, share anecdotes from research and your own experience that emphasize potential and growth. Use the resources listed in Appendix A for book clubs, professional learning communities, or simply subjects for coffee talks and PTA meetings.

- Be a model of practice and persistence. Share the challenges you face and how you will practice to overcome them. Share how you will work to learn a new language, get in better shape, or budget your time better to make sure you can spend time in your garden. Above all, do not share your weaknesses as challenges that are out of your control or hopeless. Your students are listening—both to your intended messages and your unintended communications.

- Give meaningful, specific encouragement for effort. When students do well at a task, ask them how they did so. Even if your first conversations continue to result in, "I don't know, I just did," keep helping students understand the concrete steps they took to be successful. As students see your appreciation for the steps they took to be successful, they internalize the value of process. If the goal is to help students generalize good work habits to other situations, giving authentic feedback should be a primary tool.

Meaningful Practice in the Classroom

Establishing a framework for learning in the classroom and school will help educators fully tap into the potential growth of students that meaningful practice provides. This framework for learning is entirely dependent on the expertise of the teacher, and is an enhancement to any curriculum, instruction, or standards you are responsible for in your school or district. The following concepts are a place to start:

- **Guide and support learning.** Pearson and Gallagher (1983) first proposed a model for gradually releasing the responsibility for learning from teacher to student. As deep understanding depends on multiple exposures to a topic or concept, they propose a structure for ensuring that instruction moves students towards independence. Many educators have adapted and internalized this structure as follows:
  - First, "I do." The teacher provides example or instruction through direct instruction. Let's call this first stage *exposure*.
  - Next, "We do." Students work with the teacher to complete tasks associated with learning the concept. Let's call this stage *process review*.
  - Finally, "You do," both in small groups and individually. Let's call this stage *practice*, with an eye towards independence and mastery.

Using these stages helps ensure key concepts will be thoroughly covered. Coaching students in both the content and the instructional stage will help them better attend to the information being presented. How is exposure work different than process review work? How is practice for mastery different than process review? If students understand that they can (and should!) be asking questions and seeking out help during the process review stage but should be largely independent by the practice stage, they internalize important learning strategies. When planning for student learning, consider the following:

- **Identify specific learning objectives and work backwards.** Any framework for learning depends on reflection, especially in terms of lesson effectiveness. If during lesson planning, you are able to give a concise, clear answer as to why each aspect of your lesson or unit will help students better understand a concept, you will be better able to clearly communicate those learning objectives to students. Explicitly stating and visibly recording learning objectives for all students to see helps them answer the question, "Why are we doing this?"

- **Assess the clarity of your lesson objectives.** How do you assess the clarity of your lesson objectives? Ask a colleague to circulate during your class and ask students why they are doing what they are doing. If the answer is, "because my teacher told me to," you have work to do! The potential for student success is increased when they know the purpose behind their assignment.
- **Build students' background knowledge of process.** Coaching students on assignment meaning and purpose is not limited to content; students of all ages must have guidance on the structure of work and practice. When students have sufficient background knowledge, they are far more likely to be successful.

When preparing to take on an independent task, are students able to:

- Identify the purpose or objective of the assignment?
- Identify what level of expertise the assignment requires and the ramifications of that level? For example, "This is an exposure assignment. I am going to preview this chapter for tomorrow's class. I know this should take me 15–20 minutes and if I don't understand something, it is fine, because this is the first time I am seeing this information and I can ask questions tomorrow. In fact, I should use post-it notes to record any big questions I might have!"
- Understand and use the background knowledge they have in order to be successful?

Keeping track of how students use their background knowledge of process, while a daunting task, is a powerful instructional tool. One way is to have students track their time on task with a graphic similar to the one shown in Figure 3.1. The graphic can be placed at the top of each homework assignment. Based on your knowledge of your students, you can indicate the amount of time that students likely will need to complete the task. Students can then compare the actual time they took to complete the task with the estimate that you have provided.

Fig. 3.1. Tracking my learning

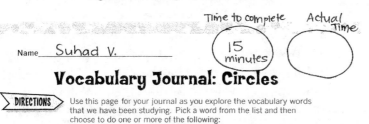

Name Suhad V.

Time to complete: 15 minutes

Actual Time

Vocabulary Journal: Circles

> DIRECTIONS: Use this page for your journal as you explore the vocabulary words that we have been studying. Pick a word from the list and then choose to do one or more of the following:

When a student's actual time on task is significantly discrepant from the teacher's estimate, it affords the student and teacher a great opportunity to discuss why. Future assignments can then be adjusted for length, or abandoned due to ease. Collecting class data is an excellent way to double-check your expectations with students.

Using Expectations and Emphasis to Motivate

A language is an exact reflection of the character and growth of its speakers. —Gandhi, 1928

Conversations with students about their work are a mainstay of effective teaching and coaching. Dweck's (2006) studies show us that putting emphasis on the hard work that students do and encouraging them to struggle in order to face and conquer challenges are effective ways to motivate students to do well. There are other messages teachers can convey in their conversations with students to motivate them.

- **Find out who students identify with and remind them that they can emulate those individuals.** Students who know of even one person who is like them in some way and who is doing what they want to do—someone who made it—will get the message that there is a real possibility for their success.

- **Do not make things too easy or comfortable.** That is not to say that students should be made to suffer, but it seems that learners are more motivated when they can see that they do not yet have it all, but they could. Coyle (2009) writes, "Being highly motivated, when you think about it, is a slightly irrational state. One forgoes comfort now in order to work toward some bigger prospective benefit later on" (106). In exploring what he called "talent hotbeds," he noticed they all were a lot like the van down by the river (as observed by Matt Foley, Chris Farley's Saturday Night Live motivational speaker). These hotbeds of talent were austere, and sometimes even run-down. The places were not beautifully decorated. This analogy can help students see the contrast between their situation and that of the people they emulate. In most schools, this will not be difficult to integrate naturally into the average school day.

- **Make sure students know that they are fortunate.** This might seem to contradict the idea above, but even without state-of-the-art equipment in gorgeous surroundings, in most situations students can be helped to perceive the opportunities they have. If students see that what they are being offered is not something that everyone else gets—whether it is the chance to use a piece of equipment, play an instrument, or join a team—they will clearly see its value.

- **Give them a sense of belonging.** A feeling of belonging now or in the future can give students the motivation to work hard. A provocative study of motivation suggests that, "...even aspects that may seem personal and unique, such as long-held attitudes, are socially transmitted and even shared" (Walton and Cohen 2011, 80). Putting an unmotivated student in a motivated group is one way to accomplish this. And students who have found someone to emulate may already feel a sense of belonging to the role model's group. Making sure students have realistic heroes and giving them opportunities to find out about them can kindle a student's will to achieve success.

Moving Forward

A resource list can be found in Appendix A. Educators can use it as a springboard for their own studies and discovery about the usefulness of findings from cognitive science in shaping teaching and learning. Likely, there is not a single educator on the planet who is looking for something extra to fill their empty day. Fortunately, many of the ideas found in these resources can inform and fit into almost any existing classroom curriculum and instruction. Most educators are already doing some of this. Being aware of the cognitive science behind the choices we make helps us internalize a stronger philosophy of education, which in turn brings about an increase in on-target responses to the thousands of decisions we have to make in real time each day.

Thinking and Teaching in 2.0: Getting Others in on the Conversation

Growth mindset. Neuroplasticity. The power of meaningful practice. Each of these concepts encompasses a powerful, newly tapped, and better understood potential for students and teachers in any classroom. Pick the most intriguing of these three concepts and consider how you would tackle the following tasks:

- Facilitate a conversation about your chosen concept at a faculty meeting.

- Create a short, kid-friendly activity to introduce students to the concept.

- Make a short presentation to a school board to garner support for a specific curriculum project featuring this concept.

- Develop a resource for parents that helps them become partners in fostering the concept.

- Start a wiki, blog, or social media page to encourage online discussion of the concept with colleagues at other schools and around the country.

Chapter 4

Professional Learning Relationships in Schools

Ruminations

In the current world culture, especially online, equality is a pervasive theme. Wired educators in any part of the world can share lesson plans, philosophies, and solutions. Unionized educators are striving for an equal share of power and greater collaboration in policy and decision-making. Professional and amateur writers have equal access to readers because of blogs and other Web 2.0 tools. Students and teachers have equal access to information, and equal opportunity to share it. In this, there are exciting possibilities—the richness of new points of view, a greater diversity of ideas in our conversations, and the promise of new approaches to problem solving.

To be fair, there are also many challenges. An open opportunity to find and share information does not necessarily translate to an equal ability to contextualize, analyze, or understand it.

The flip side of the phenomenon of wired equality is the lack of a gatekeeper. How do we know if the amateur writer's facts are complete and accurate? How can we be sure the student's information is accurate? More importantly, how can a student be sure that the information gathered from Internet sources is correct or appropriate? How do we know if a website is not just a good-looking collection of urban legends? If we are fortunate as a society, we will be able to continue to depend on the expertise of reference librarians to help us with fact-checking. But in these times, anyone who uses the Internet must embrace the attitude of a good fact checker: curiosity blended with a healthy dose of skepticism. We have to develop the accompanying skills as well, and then we have to pass this mindset and these skills on to our students. We all need to be aware that some facts are more equal than others.

Some Facts Are More Equal than Others

The world of Web 2.0 offers an array of services beyond the set products available in Web 1.0. For example, we can now post our photos to Flickr™, a user-generated content management system, rather than purchasing a digital-to-paper photo processing service. Knobel and Wilber (2009) describe three interlocking functions or practices that characterize Web 2.0: participation, collaboration, and distribution. Online services for managing user-generated content enable anyone to participate in the production of media and to respond to content that others have generated. Blogs and fan fiction sites are familiar examples. Collaboration is evident in online multiuser writing and remix spaces, such as wikis or multiplayer online games. Digital networks and hosting spaces provide distribution resources. Consequently, individuals can use sites like YouTube™ to share their knowledge, expertise, and experiences that sometimes border on sheer nonsense, but are highly appealing to many viewers. More than likely, many students (if not all) have engaged in activities that involve each of these Web 2.0 practices. Later in this chapter, we provide a list of Web 2.0 collaboration tools.

Teaching students to ferret out which sources of online information provide solid evidence, how to identify bias, and key strategies for separating commercially influenced information from factual research may be among the most important tools students develop in 21st century classrooms. As social networking services, online ratings and reviews, blogging, and mobile phone applications continue to increase the interconnectedness between citizens and content, students cannot be left unprepared for a world that is going to map their digital footprints.

When it comes to putting the *I* in *Internet*, current (and for the moment, foreseeable future) programs, applications, queries, searches, and marketing campaigns are squarely aimed at getting individual users to personally interact with and influence the content they are consuming. Check in where you travel! Rate your purchase! Tag your favorite friends in the photos you took this weekend!

Why is this trend deserving of our attention? As students leave high school for college and the workplace, the digital footprints (or lack thereof) they leave behind can significantly influence their ability to live the future they dream of and desire. Students' futures will not be solely defined by how they live and learn in their classrooms and communities; it will also be influenced by their online presence.

Our ability to connect and work together online is but one small facet of why collaboration is important to our 21st century students. If educators are to prepare students for careers that depend on human interaction more than ever before, it is not enough to talk the talk. They must practice what they aim to teach their students about working together, beginning in their own classrooms and schools.

The Professional Learning Network

Balancing the attitude of open-minded wired equality with that of cautious fact-checking must be the new model for all relationships in schools. Consider the role of participation and relationships in such school-based scenarios as these:

- A teacher in a professional learning network who wants to know why it is important for a class group to number six or fewer students in order for her to be effective in facilitating catch-up growth for those who are behind.

- A principal who is trying to winnow down a list of potential resources for a school improvement team to review regarding a supplemental mathematics intervention curriculum.

- A teacher who is skeptical of the claims of a researched-based program the principal is suggesting for reading instruction.

- A student who questions how it is we know that the sun is made mostly of helium when no one can get close enough to take a sample.

When life is good and relationships are healthy, trust exists among the people, in every one of those situations. And, when life is good and relationships are healthy, the questioning nature of the skeptic must not just be tolerated, but embraced as a role that strengthens our convictions rather than weakening them.

Emerson (1849) wrote of being a transparent eyeball—seeing and observing without ego. It seems that in professional learning networks—with grade-level and content-area colleagues, and with policy-makers at all levels—a similar feat is required of educators. Planning for instruction is not about favorite units. Solving problems is not about addressing pet peeves. Leadership is not about "my way of doing things." However, approaching new ideas without ego is not the same as approaching them without standards. Effective collaboration requires balancing those same sophisticated skills: Open curiosity with skepticism. Fortunately there are more and more models of successful collaboration for us to draw upon (Baccellieri 2010; DuFour and Marzano 2011; Garmston and Wellman 2008).

Perhaps it is the hard wind of economic pressure that has brought out the need for collaboration in such sharp relief. Maybe the problems and responsibilities that teaching brings today are more demanding now than ever before. Has educational policy done it? Or is social change the source? However we choose to address the important issues we face in our classrooms and schools, two heads are usually better than one, and three heads are probably even better than two. An old saying in Jerry's family is, "If you think there are two sides to every story, you have probably missed a few sides." With stronger frameworks for collaborative input come greater transparency; this transparency in our planning helps keep us honest, on our toes, and more focused on clear objectives.

These three important concepts are crucial in developing a dynamic and productive collaborative process:

- Collaboration is not merely an educational prerogative; it is an economic necessity.
- Considering diverse perspectives is not easy, especially when participants have different fundamental beliefs.
- Understanding the difference between toolbox diversity (the skills and expertise different individuals can bring to a group) and diverse preferences (the values and belief systems represented by the individuals in a group) is essential in building collaborative teams (Page 2007).

Economic Necessity

Whether we are exploring globalization through the power of social networking, video conferencing, or predicting new markets or supply sources overseas, our future personal and economic potential is inextricably linked to how cultures contact and collide with one another all around the world. In past years, business leaders who were transferred to overseas posts often viewed their moves as demotions. Today, experience in international markets is not only preferable, it is deemed essential for those leading large corporations and non-profit organizations.

If collaboration is one of the engines driving our economic potential, then it is not enough to simply tolerate other cultures, beliefs, and practices. We must move our character education curricula beyond tolerance and move our students towards accepting and understanding differences in order to successfully navigate professional life in the 21st century. The training and human resources departments of Fortune 500 companies now regularly incorporate diversity training into standard coursework and preparation for new and experienced employees alike. They cannot afford not to be prepared for effective collaboration between employees and customers.

Dealing with Differences

In building his case for the power of diversity in building collaborative groups for problem-solving, Page (2007) aptly notes, "Interacting with a large number of diverse people should be more cognitively taxing than hanging out with your close friends, who look, think, and act just like you" (xiv–xv). Although the Internet gives us the ability to seek out all kinds of ideas and concepts that challenge our view of the world, we are more likely to seek out those that share our vision. Our Web browsers do not help with our elucidation, either, as search engine heuristics are programmed to send us links and suggestions that we are likely to find more appealing with every click or selection we make.

As we work with others, the differences in our values are often like an unspoken weight hanging above our heads. During much of the so-called reading wars (whole language vs. phonics) and mathematics wars (traditional American rote memorization vs. reform-based math using manipulatives and concepts only), well-meaning educators with stark fundamental differences were pitted against one another. Discourse often descended into vitriol, often scuttling any chance at finding common ground. Thankfully, as teachers and researchers alike find balance in both theory and practice, the pendulum swings tend to lessen and students benefit from careful and reflective thoughts which harness the best thinking from multiple perspectives. In this fashion, we can ensure that we avoid debates that encourage a winner-take-all scenario, and work to build win-win situations for students and teachers.

Toolbox Diversity

Imagine that you are a biologist or an economist working with systems in nature or the market. What qualities would you look for in defining a healthy ecosystem or portfolio? It is an environment that contains a single species which depends on a single source of nutrition, disconnected from the rest of the food chain? It is an investment strategy that puts all of the financial resources of an economy into a single market sector or financial product? We have seen the results of relying on sub-prime mortgages as an engine for economic growth. The strongest systems are built on diversity.

Page (2007) takes great care to define how diversity influences group performance: how unpacking the tools we use in problem-solving into specific frameworks, including how we interpret or categorize perspectives, how we generate solutions, and how we infer cause and effect when making predictions. Bringing teams together to examine best practices in education and how they apply to their classrooms and schools will be more successful if these teams bring a rich collection of experiences and expertise to the table. For example, if they are examining school-wide discipline policies in an elementary school, it would be crucial to have representation from teachers of different age groups and curricular areas, as well as paraprofessionals (aides, playground supervisors and custodians), as each participant will bring a different perspective on what are appropriate expectations for children in various school settings.

Collaboration brings a sense of unity to our professional relationships. In the current educational climate—in which those with power and the bullies can make statements that simultaneously dismiss the wisdom that educators gain with experience, and gainsay the well-supported conclusions of brain science that experience builds expertise—it is important that educators work together. If professional learning relationships are built on a foundation of trust, members can disagree in a constructive way. They can have confidence that underneath any perceived philosophical leanings, the solutions proposed are in students' best interests.

Processing and More Processing

Have you ever noticed that among all of your state's standards, goals, and descriptors—there are process standards? Any classroom teachers who are responsible for teaching science will be familiar with the science goals that deal with the concepts of life, physical, earth, and space sciences that students should know. Most likely these are the areas teachers bookmark on their browser.

But dig a little bit deeper, and you are likely to find such goals as "Inquiry and Design" and "Science, Technology and Society" which seem like unexplored territory when contrasted with the familiar neighborhood of the content area outlines. One example of a state's process or inquiry goal is for students to "Understand the processes of scientific inquiry and technological design to investigate questions, conduct experiments, and solve problems." Among the many standards listed under this goal, students are supposed to be able to:

- formulate possible solutions to a given design problem in early elementary school.
- use data to produce reasonable explanations in late elementary school.
- report and display the process and results of a scientific investigation in junior high school (Illinois State Board of Education).

It seems like a safe bet to note that a teacher would be able to clearly state the science content goals her students are supposed to explore during the school year and describe the activities the students do in order to explore them.

Unfortunately, it would also be a safe bet to state that the same teacher would not be able to describe how, over a series of lessons, she would go about helping her students to become better at formulating possible solutions to design problems; or, what the scope and sequence looks like for helping students produce reasonable explanations; or, the workshop she attended that helped her better teach students to collaborate in order to report and display results of scientific investigations.

Effective teaching in the 21st century must integrate these sophisticated processes into the curriculum. And, there must be plenty of opportunities for students to practice. Collaboration provides those opportunities. Collaboration, among other 21st century skills, is essential to "all students today, not just an elite few." However, learning how to collaborate is "rarely incorporated deliberately throughout the curriculum, nor [is it] routinely assessed" (Kay 2010).

Why is this crucial piece missing from educational practice? It is not because teachers have been remiss. It is not that the goals and standards are inappropriate—if anything, these goals and standards are ahead of their time! This piece is missing because the times have rapidly changed. Everyone knows this, but it is technology, like the flashy younger sibling, that keeps getting everyone's attention. We are finally seeing the importance of the quiet, dependable older sibling: connectedness. Yet fostering connectedness is far more complex than ordering interactive whiteboards, and education has not caught up…Yet, that is.

Learning Networks Are Not Just for Colleagues Anymore

Coyle (2009) says that one of the marks of a great teacher is "the matrix," a deep understanding of the subject matter they are teaching. But there must be more in the matrix than just content. Knowledge about the learning process must be woven through the matrix as well so that teachers know how to troubleshoot when a student runs into obstacles. If one approach does not work, the teacher can try many others. Great teachers are aware of the bits and parts of which a skill or concept is made. They understand those bits and parts. They also understand the process of integrating those pieces.

More and more, educators are getting firsthand experience of what school is like for their students. The learning curve for us is getting steeper and steeper because the profession requires more and more from its practitioners. We are required to put aside preconceived ideas, search for new ones, share them, try them, make judgments about their effectiveness, and mold the new with the old. Just as in a garden, healthy growth requires the planting, pruning, and fertilization of ideas.

As educators engage in the gradual, frustrating, exhilarating, and constant process of learning, their matrix about how humans learn widens and deepens. The paradigm shift educators need to make is that, in order to be expert teachers, they must become experts at the messy business of learning. Their confidence, built on their successes and experience, needs a healthy dose of missteps, trials, and tribulations so that they can become learning partners with their students.

In this context, the classroom becomes a learning network. And, as the teachers are likely the most competent learners in the classrooms, they can model what it is like to encounter new information. Students need to witness expert learners, undaunted by the challenges and failures that authentic learning brings. It is a healthy struggle that makes learning possible, not effortless displays of knowledge and ability. As students discover that struggle is necessary in order to progress, educators will discover that the student learning process parallels their own.

Collaboration between students—and without us—is also crucial to our students' learning because the collective knowledge of our planet has consistently grown over the centuries. The poplulation, cultural, and economic growth over the past two decades has been astounding. Karl Fisch's (2007) thought-provoking "Did You Know?" YouTube video (originally developed as a Microsoft PowerPoint™ for a high school faculty meeting in 2006, with over 13 million views as of March 2011) illuminates a number of challenges we face today. Among these challenges are the following:

- We are educating students to be prepared for jobs and new technologies that do not yet exist.
- Technical information evolves so rapidly that half of what students learn in their first year of studies is already out of date by their third year in college.
- The top in-demand jobs of 2010 did not exist in 2004.

An updated view of collaboration is not simply a matter of best practices in education, but is vital to our students' future success (Himmele and Himmele 2011). Our students are no longer simply consumers of information, they are the mass distributors.

Organizational Frameworks to Support Collaboration

Learning how to collaborate and set realistic goals is not unlike learning good posture, which often does not feel right at first. Models and frameworks for collaboration abound in print. Finding the right one can make all the difference in the world, especially as your collaboration becomes action-oriented, rather than simply another meeting spent admiring the challenges you face.

As federal and state funding makes the transition from No Child Left Behind to Race to the Top, the stakes for schools' and districts' annual improvement plans continue to get higher and higher. Each entity frequently correlates these formal, required plans to the goals and standards of the organizations that oversee their progress and development. These plans become a map not unlike the traditional spiritual Dem Bones, where the school goals are connected to the district goals, the district goals are connected to the state standards, and if, as expected, many state standards will connect to the Common Core State Standards Initiative (2010). Little imagination is needed to notice that educators often find themselves facing a long list of directives that all have high levels of importance and urgency. Responding effectively to such mandates requires application of what we describe as *The Ls*: Listening to others, Leadership sharing, and Lifelong Learning commitment.

Which restaurant menu is easier for you to digest—the one presented in a ring binder with pages of salads, sandwiches, pizzas, pastas, and other entrees, or the one page menu with a limited number of thoughtful selections relating to a common theme or two? It is our job as the instructional leaders of our schools and districts to keep our focus on strategic and realistic improvement. When faced with a dizzying array of options, we must identify what we can do well in a timely fashion and what will deserve (and need) a long-term organizational plan. It does not matter whether we are chunking information on a micro (reading a technical article) or macro (planning a school's direction for the coming school year) level; once our list of items is longer than we can easily recall, chances are any one item on that list will not get the full attention it deserves.

Collaboration is the key to navigating this challenge. We would argue that to begin any planning for important institutional change, all involved constituents should share a common language, framework, and understanding for an established collaborative process. In fact, establishing this framework may be the first step in building an effective school improvement team and plan. In Figure 4.1, a sample listing of objectives illustrates how a framework for supporting a learning environment precedes probing deeper pedagogical concerns.

Fig. 4.1. School Improvement Plan

Primary objectives for years one through three

Year One
• Establish common language and framework(s) for running school improvement, problem-solving team (academic and behavioral), and school discipline committee meetings
• Identify collaboration as the key theme and strategy for the school year
• Pilot a math intervention program in targeted primary and intermediate classrooms

Year Two
• Implement frameworks for academic interventions (Response to Intervention—RTL) and behavioral interventions (Positive Behavior Supports—PBS)
• Expand math intervention program to all classrooms at each grade level with professional development support through coaching
• Study how learning objectives are shared with students and how student performance is affected by the ways in which those objectives are shared

Year Three
• Examine and review effectiveness of frameworks for RTL and PBS, supporting suggested changes through professional development and peer-to-peer collaboration
• Establish professional learning communities focused on addressing issues raised during study of school standards and practice in order to establish learning objectives
• Evaluate effectiveness of math intervention program

Rather than taking on multiple content areas at a time, this plan narrows its focus to one content area. Woven into the strategic development is time spent on the systems that will support future efforts. As these school leaders shape which actions they will take, they take care to have teachers using the same language, expectations, and tools for communication. Although some of the tools and standards may seem to artificially limit initial conversations, greater efficiency and positive results will help make the process feel more meaningful and worthwhile. As any veteran of a problem-solving or student support team can attest, the less time we spend admiring the problem, the better. Results reduce stress better than any conversation can.

Among the many models and philosophies for developing and implementing continuous school improvement, the key is finding one that matches the needs of your team, school, or district. Regardless of how a school organizes for successful professional learning communities, develops SMART (Specific, Measurable, Action-oriented, Realistic, and Time-bound) goals, or uses a protocol for running effective meetings, if collaboration is to be a centerpiece for both student and teacher learning, certain qualities must be in place. These frameworks or protocols must foster listening to others' voices to develop shared leadership in order to solve the challenges that we regularly face when trying to develop lifelong learning in all of our students.

Listening to Others

Despite the ostensible effectiveness of any instruction, it can be enhanced by positive student-teacher relationships (Marzano 2011). When teachers take an active interest in students' lives, their advocacy for students is enhanced, and that helps students feel the power of a friendly relationship. This is true of collegial relationships, too. One of the first questions teachers often ask before joining a committee charged with making important school decisions is, "Will my voice be heard and taken seriously?" Making the purposeful decision to dedicate time and energy to listening ensures that a high value is placed on the members of the team and their collective experience, knowledge, and wisdom. And, even though the move towards common standards for all states to share focuses primarily on content standards, the Common Core

Standards Initiative (2010) still notes that, "Whatever their intended major or profession, high school graduates will depend heavily on their ability to listen attentively to others so that they are able to build on others' meritorious ideas while expressing their own clearly and persuasively."

Shared Leadership

Honest collaboration depends on equal input. Equal input builds a collective trust in the final decision, even if all members are forced to compromise. When teams know they have more than one "go-to" person, confidence is dispersed to a wider range of formal and informal leaders. Unity behind a common goal is also the most effective way to build enduring trust in a learning community, as everyone has a personal stake in being successful.

Developing Habits of Lifelong Learning

If there is anything that the 21st century has already taught us, it is that change is an ever-increasing constant. Careers are now built on an ever-shifting and changing array of tools that must be quickly mastered to stay current and marketable in today's economy. Experience matters, but so does your capacity for growth and change. Our beliefs, habits, and actions influence our students and their potential, so we must always be forever pushing the bar higher for ourselves, just as we do for our students.

Collaboration Is Key

Today, articles online and in print that make unfavorable comparisons between school systems in the United States and elsewhere are ubiquitous. Lost in the finger-pointing is one indisputable fact: other successful education systems give teachers more time to plan and collaborate (Darling-Hammond et al. 2009). Time for teamwork and preparation is built into the day rather than left as an afterthought.

We must purposefully build time into our days for collaboration; we must purposefully build structures to make that collaboration meaningful. When our students (or colleagues) seem as if they might prefer to work alone, we need to remind ourselves how cognitively taxing it can be to work with groups of divergent thinkers with different fundamental belief systems (Page 2007).

As no one can possibly know all the important information all by themselves, much less know what to do with it, collaboration clearly is the key to identifying and marshaling the information and processes needed to solve a challenge. The sheer amount of information and interconnectedness in present society makes demands on our attention that are increasingly impossible to resist. Consequently, we must develop strategies to streamline and share that pertinent information effectively. Collaboration is the process by which all of us are able to further our expertise and to judge which facts are more equal than others. In a world economy that shifts with great speed, being able to communicate what makes an idea important is invaluable.

Web 2.0 Collaboration Tools

Here are some great ways to collaborate using the Internet. All these tools allow people to work together, whether they are in the same room or not. Collaboration tools on the web seem to fall into five general categories. Appendix B contains a list of these resources and their URLs.

Online Meeting/Communication

- **Skype™**: Skype allows users to make video calls through the Internet. It is free as long as the other user is also using Skype™.
- **Google Talk™**: This is a free application for instant messaging and voice-over Internet protocol (VOIP).

Backchannels

A backchannel includes all of the ideas that are not coming from the presenter in the room. In the "old days," we would pass notes and whisper. Now, it is possible to use the backchannel to help students communicate and collaborate. They can add to the discussion. Backchannels can be complex or simple, in real time or not. They come in many forms. The following are just a few:

- TodaysMeet©
- backchan.nl®
- Wallwisher©

Information Sharing

- **Diigo©**: This dynamic bookmarking and annotating service allows users to share virtual sticky-notes, highlights, and running commentary for online articles and information.
- **Delicious©**: This service allows you to organize bookmarks.
- **Digg©**: This is a website that allows people to share Internet content. They can also find, vote, and comment on links and stories that others have submitted.

Online Classrooms/Multipurpose Group Managers

These services provide a multitude of features, all of which allow the user to communicate, track, and organize. The features might include shared lesson plans, a plan book, a grade book, the ability to screencast, video publishing, live online classes, integration with Twitter© or Facebook, online quizzes and tests, homework submission and grading, and chat rooms.

- Udemy©
- Moodle™
- Edmodo©
- Wiggio©
- Brainhoney©

Project and Document Collaboration

- **Google Docs**: This online document manager allows groups of people to simultaneously access, view, edit, and organize documents, spreadsheets, presentations, and more. Once users are logged in, they can also communicate via a chat window while editing or viewing a document.

- **Wikispaces©**: A wiki functions as both a website and a document editor. But it is a collaborative effort and the document can include embedded videos, links, and images. Wikipedia®, for example, is a wiki. Wikispaces allows teachers to create a wiki with students.

- **Mind42.com©**: This browser-based online application allows you to collaboratively make a mind-map. Like Wikispaces, the mind-map can include videos, links, and images.

- **Gliffy©**: This is another browser-based online application. You can make Venn diagrams, flowcharts, and floor plans, among several other types of graphic organizers.

Thinking and Teaching in 2.0: School 2.0, Can You Hear Me Now?

"Coming together is a beginning. Keeping together is progress. Working together is success." —Henry Ford (n.d.)

Honoring the time and effort it takes to make collaboration authentic and effective is an important aspect of any school or district's professional learning community. What does collaboration look like in your school? How does it directly influence student learning? Try these ideas to start thinking about ways to enhance collaboration in your school:

- Choose one of the 2.0 collaboration tools as a way to explore a theme or idea for a unit or content area with your colleagues. Treat it more like a brainstorming session rather than a detailed planner. What did you learn about the content? What did you learn about the tool?

- Consider sharing with your students how you plan, and collaborate with colleagues. Share templates, wikis, or any other organizational tools you use. How might this influence their attitudes towards collaboration?

- Ormiston (2011) maintains that technology supports collaboration among students. She states, "By allowing students to choose, within defined parameters, what and how to study, teachers encourage students to study in ways that most effectively engage them with the content.... Web 2.0 tools can facilitate collaboration, which means, for example, that teachers need to explore ways that social networking can be adapted for teaching and learning" (30). In what ways do Ormiston's observations reflect your thinking or that of your colleagues?

Chapter 5

Connecting Meaningful Learning to the Power of Practice

Ruminations

It is an age-old conundrum. Why is it that the child who will spend countless hours trying to perfect a single trick on her skateboard will insist that the written portion of her project on friction is done after a single draft? Why does the student who persistently tracks his savings and calculates how long it will take him to save up for an MP3 player balk at practicing his math facts? While few will argue the value of practice, finding ways to make it meaningful for each of the students in our care can be an arduous task, even in the best of classroom climates.

Clearly, this skater and music lover have a personal investment in the goal they are trying to accomplish. Athletes and musicians have a vested interest in practice. Whether on a court or field, stage or studio, their continued success is based on their ability to perform. Those with the greatest expertise are not those lucky enough to pull a rabbit out of a hat on game day; when it is time to perform, they are trying to replicate what they have already done in practice for hours each day over a period of many years.

Many students who fall short of success do so not because of issues of ability, but because of issues of motivation and stamina. In Chapter 3, we looked at the science behind the potential each of our brains has for learning and development, the influence of teachers, the significance of possessing a growth mindset (Dweck 2006; 2010), and an introductory framework for how to use this information in classroom instruction. In this chapter, we elaborate on this framework by connecting information about learning and brain development to classroom practices that engage students as well as strengthen their resolve. Specifically, we describe the kind of language that best encourages students, and classroom routines that promote learning progress.

The Relationship between Effective Teaching and Effective Learning

Simply stated, there are three reasons for reading: for enjoyment, to learn something, and when required to. Learning, in the more general sense, can also be perceived in this way. Teachers and students alike often overlook the third reason: because you have to. Why? Probably because it does not seem like a good reason to read and learn until, of course, you want to pass your driver's license test. In order to address the latter two situations—to learn and for having to complete specific tasks—teachers give assignments to students.

Assignments are a staple of the daily diet in a typical classroom. And when the assignment does not resonate with the students as a result of their curiosity and interest, they might not have a clear understanding of its purpose. Even details in the assignment that are intended to increase engagement might end up obscuring the original learning objective. For example, a word problem about the average number of downloads per day from popular music groups might lead students to discuss their favorite artist rather than lead them to solve the problem.

As a result, it is easy to conclude that assignments hinder learning or are unnecessary (Cushman 2010). After all, children are naturally curious. In an enriched environment, they will learn by exploring, using the available resources, and asking questions. But this conclusion is not conducive to universal learning in schools. Our students are children. Children do not usually have the experience, perspective, and wide-ranging knowledge that adults tend to have. Human childhood lasts an almost absurdly long time when compared to the juvenile stage in other mammals. For example, gorilla females are ready to have babies of their own at about eight years old. But the long duration of human childhood is necessary because becoming a successful adult human is a difficult and complex process.

Instead of concluding that all assignments hamper learning because they did not come from student interests—or going to the other extreme and giving assignments with complete disregard to student interest because of the dictates of the curriculum—it would be more constructive to consider the interaction between students' inherent interests and the demands of the curriculum. Excellent teachers harness the dynamic relationship between the two.

This situation is much like the dynamic interaction between genes and environment that David Shenk (2010) describes in his book *The Genius in All of Us: Why Everything You've Been Told About Genetics, Talent, and IQ Is Wrong*. He updates the common, outdated Mendelian view that the way our genes are expressed is summed up by the phrase "nature vs. nurture." A common misconception is that genes determine all of a person's traits, and environment comes in afterward with a little fine-tuning. He goes on to explain, "There is no genetic foundation that gets laid before the environment enters in; rather, genes express themselves strictly in accordance with their environment" (18). In other words, the environment influences whether a gene is expressed, and to what extent.

Shenk (2010) gives an example of a study that compared Japanese children raised in California to those raised in Japan. Although they share the same gene pool, the children raised in California were an average of five inches taller. Height is commonly seen as determined by genes alone, but clearly nutrition and other environmental factors influence this trait.

This realization is an important distinction for educators. "We do not inherit traits directly from our genes. Instead, we develop traits through the dynamic process of gene-environment interaction" (Shenk 2010, 18). Like the expression of genes, the expression of a student's interests is malleable. Interests are influenced by many environmental factors—classmates' interests and opinions, books they are encouraged to check out, experiences at home, what is read aloud to them, television shows, conversations with others, family pastimes, current events, a teacher's digressions, and a plethora of other variables. Just as current research updates our understanding of genes and environment, we can update our view of the role that student interest plays in instructional decisions.

When an assignment originates from outside sources, such as the teachers or curriculum, and not from the interest of the student—it is the environment in our classrooms that can make the difference between a student merely going through the motions—(playing Simon Says)—and having an authentic learning experience.

Understanding Why Is Half the Battle

During a typical week at school, students participate in a range of activities including writing workshop, guided practice in math class, or content-area reading in preparation for a discussion or activity. In the course of these activities, they might receive such instructions as these:

- Make sure you complete a rough draft of your narrative this week.

- Sort the triangles into three categories: scalene, isosceles, and equilateral.
- Read the first section of this chapter to learn more about Jamestown, and write the main idea of each paragraph on a sticky note.

If the meanings of the academic vocabulary such as *rough draft*, *narrative*, *triangle*, *scalene*, *isosceles*, *equilateral*, and *main idea* have been developed well enough in class to ensure that the students understand them, then each direction is clear and concise. And, the students might do a stellar job at following directions and finishing an assignment within the parameters prescribed. But that does not equate to learning.

If a student's answer to "What are you working on?" is "Page 305," there might be a little cause for concern. Dig a little deeper. If, upon asking for further elaboration as to why he is working on page 305, the answer is, "Because the teacher told me to," then the locus for learning is out of whack. There might be a great reason for why page 305 appears at this point in the curriculum, but that reason has yet to resonate with this learner.

Some students already have their own learning goals. Short of that, the locus for learning finds its way inside the students in two ways: inspiration and aspiration. Students can be inspired by something in their environment—a fellow classmate, a successful experience, or a teacher—that makes them soar to greater heights. Or, they might value a learning goal now because of something they aspire to later in their lives.

In *The Talent Code: Greatness Isn't Born*, Daniel Coyle (2009) refers to a sense of future belonging. For example, Julian knows that at some time in the future, he wants to be able to work on cars—fix them, tune them up, or rebuild their engines. He knows he cannot do it yet. He knows that he needs to be bigger, stronger, and slightly richer than he is now. But, he might not know how important it is that he understands fractions so he can successfully choose sockets for his wrenches or gap a spark plug. If we get to know Julian well enough to know that about him, and let him in on the fact that fraction concepts are a necessary part of his chosen future, the learning goal is likely to become Julian's. Making sure that the locus for learning is inside the learner is arguably the most important job that a teacher has.

Foundations for Effective Teaching

What qualities define an effective teacher? To turn a phrase, effectiveness can be in the eye of the beholder. In order to attempt to be more objective, Reeves (2003) favors frequent evaluations created by teams of teachers specifically for their students and curriculum. Such evaluations allow these teachers to accurately determine if their students are learning. Careful analysis will help them to hone the educational practices that are most likely to bring about learning. Although corporations have attempted this approach on a vast scale to improve productivity and the bottom line, the end result for teachers differs. The goal for teachers and those who support them is to gain some insight into effective practices for their students and curriculum. Frequent assessment of progress on specific goals focuses the lens through which we view our challenges.

Our goal is to look at qualities that help teachers and students understand the science and strategies that help them build expertise. We do not claim that this list is exhaustive; it is merely a starting point to begin the conversation and the learning. Foundations for teaching that promote the development of student expertise include:

- developing relationships with students that balance a respect for learning with a personal interest in the student's well-being and educational development
- teaching and classroom language that focuses on effort over ability

- creating classroom environments that support risk-taking and learning from mistakes
- communicating learning objectives and high expectations with clarity and vision; having systems in place to make sure those objectives are understood and, in time, internalized and personalized by students
- providing frequent and multiple opportunities to show progress
- using informative data and observations to make sure learning objectives are connecting with student learning and effort

Developing positive and productive student-teacher relationships is analogous to the school-wide frameworks for promoting collaboration among colleagues described in Chapter 4. The key qualities—listening to others, developing leadership in others, and personal interest in lifelong learning and development—are equally applicable in classroom settings. Students are more likely to develop the skills and strategies they need for success in and out of school when they feel they are listened to, have opportunities to be part of leading their own learning and instruction, and are able to develop interests that keep them personally invested in improvement and learning.

The language that we use to communicate care and interest in our students' well-being can also help establish priorities in the classroom (Denton 2007; Farrell 2009; Johnston 2004). Having an atmosphere where students and teachers are willing to take risks, improve their practices, and learn from their mistakes is a critical step towards having a classroom atmosphere that promotes and celebrates thoughtful and consistent effort. Firmly establishing Dweck's "growth mindset" in students requires purposeful effort and structure, especially in a society that often incorrectly views talent as being a natural gift or innate trait. There must be an emphasis on challenge over success (Dweck 2010). How many times have you noticed students working diligently on a task, on which they know they can be successful, and, when transitioning to something more difficult, immediately become less compliant and more prone to being distracted?

Students should take pride in working on things that are harder for them, so teachers need to be advocates for perseverance in the face of adversity. Students often react to the things they cannot do as "boring" because being negative is easier than facing down fears. If we use classroom discourse to change the lens through which we view activities, we should model how we place higher intrinsic value on the things that challenge us.

If educators examine the language and discourse they use in the classroom to establish a positive learning environment, they clearly have to look carefully at what their assignments communicate to students. Learning goals and standards are often abstract to students until they help them see how to do something and why it helps them as a learner, just as we helped Julian connect fractions with his socket wrenches. Assignments are concrete vehicles for learning, and if well-designed and delivered, can lead students to better understanding of concepts that run the gamut from concrete to abstract. Moss and Brookhart (2009) sum it up well in their description of how a student should be able to express his understanding of a common comprehension instruction goal, identifying the main idea:

> What we want is more than students being able to "identify the main idea." We want students to understand that they will learn how to get a better grasp on the meaning of what they read, why that should be a goal for them, and what it feels like to do that. For the student, this means both understanding the learning goal and knowing what good work on the assignment looks like. It's not a goal if the student can't envision it (25).

It bears repeating: the student must be able to envision the goal. Students should also be able to explain why the assignment is important, and how it will help them learn.

Key ways to help students accomplish this are as follows:

- Make sure that goals are written and discussed in student-friendly language.

- Provide suitable samples of student work.
- Share student explanations of their understanding of the different quality levels in a rubric.
- Allow students to practice using a rubric to assess other samples of work (Moss and Brookhart 2009).

Expressing learning goals in student-friendly language is a task best served by collaboration with colleagues and the students themselves. Have you ever had the experience of going over a lesson's instructions or an example in your head, only to find that when you shared it out loud, it was not nearly as clear and concise as you had imagined it to be? Or, have you had a prompt that elicited great writing and discussion for two or three years, only to find that it falls flat with your current students? Sharing these experiences with colleagues and students is crucial in the ongoing process of establishing and maintaining meaningful and informative learning goals.

Through honest discussion of learning goals with our colleagues, we also participate in a practice we want to build in our classrooms: a dedication to lifelong learning, and an internal drive to hone and perfect our teaching craft. By working to improve learning goals for our students, we take an active role in continuous improvement. By sharing this process with our students, we model the significant effort it takes to improve the art and science of teaching. Simply sharing a brief anecdote such as, "I was sharing what we were doing yesterday with Ms. Collins, and she told me about a great way to better understand how a circuit works. Let me show you…" provides students with a model for collaboration and openness to new ideas. It also implies humility, demonstrating that we can turn to others in search of ideas and strategies that are better than our own.

Although a rubric can sometimes seem cumbersome, challenging to use consistently and objectively, and more time-consuming in application than other measures—it is a crucial tool. The use of a rubric facilitates regular, explicit, and useful feedback. For any tool to be effective, it must be easily understood by both the person evaluating and the person being evaluated.

One way to make rubrics more user-friendly is to search for a common metric that can be used across multiple assignments, lessons, units, or content areas. An example of a straightforward rubric for evaluating comprehension is shown in Figure 5.1.

Fig. 5.1. Comprehension strategy rubric

Rating	Description
4	You are able to use the strategy effectively to develop an accurate understanding. You can explain the steps you took, why you took them, and how these steps improved your understanding.
3	You are able to use the strategy effectively to develop a mostly accurate understanding. You can explain the steps you took to use the strategy.
2	You are able to use the strategy to develop a somewhat accurate understanding, but there are some minor inaccuracies in your work.
1	You attempt to use the strategy but do not demonstrate an accurate understanding and may have major inaccuracies in your work.

This type of rubric is an effective tool in helping students reflect about the quality of their work. Just like the use of a good graphic organizer, a rubric is a tool to help students internalize a process for successful learning. Once the process is solidly understood, regular use of the rubric is no longer needed. In this fashion, the rubric in Figure 5.1 can be used in multiple settings and across multiple content areas. Once students understand the purpose and the structure of the rubric, it helps them to understand where the finish line is for a learning goal.

Any assessment can make students wary, even when used as a pre-test for formative means. As they become familiar with the structure and routine, though, the use of a rubric that is recognizable and in student-friendly language becomes a tool that provides students greater understanding of their learning and what they need to do to improve. With greater use comes greater consistency; with greater consistency comes deeper trust. Through a gradual and, more importantly, strategic release of responsibility, students can become more adept at self-assessment. Most importantly is that they see the connection between their effort and the progress they make. The work has to be worth the effort, and the effort has to honor the work.

Reeves (2003) emphasized that the effectiveness of 90/90/90 schools was not a result of any commercial program. He noticed that these successful schools had certain characteristics in common. One of those was multiple opportunities to show progress. In order for students to be willing to take the risk to fail, they need to have multiple opportunities to succeed.

In order to make the point that while poverty can be an obstacle to academic achievement, some of its effects can still be mitigated in effective schools—Reeves created the identifier 90/90/90. He observed schools in Milwaukee, Wisconsin in 1995 that had 90% or more of students who:

- were eligible for free and reduced lunch;
- were members of ethnic minority groups; and
- met the district or state academic standards in reading or another area

Students need to receive regular, explicit feedback on their performance in order to know that the hard work they are doing is causing their progress. It is important to note that the first of the failures will be the most difficult if students have not had the feedback and the frequent opportunities to show progress in the past. They have to experience the failure-to-success process a number of times before they trust in the process and in themselves: then they will be better able to link cause—the hard work—to the effect—success.

The consistent message of the 90/90/90 schools is that the penalty for poor performance is not a low grade, followed by a forced march to the next unit. Rather, student performance that is less than proficient is followed by multiple opportunities to improve performance. Most of these schools conducted weekly assessments of student progress. It is important to note that these assessments were not district or state tests, but were assessments constructed and administered by classroom teachers. The consequence of students performing badly was not an admonishment to "Wait until next year" but rather the promise that "You can do better next week" (Reeves 2003, 4).

A Classroom Anecdote: Lisa's Story

Early spring is the time of year when math in fifth grade begins to look less like elementary school and more like junior high. In order to be able to manipulate fractions, decimals, percents, and ratios, students need to know their multiplication facts, and have good number sense. That is when it is time to differentiate like never before.

Of the three main groups in my classroom, the one I work most closely with is the one with the students who are having the most trouble. I used to think of those students as ones with less natural mathematical talent. Now, I know better. This is the group of kids who have spent less time thinking about math for all the various and sundry reasons—from sick and absent relatives inadvertently wreaking havoc in their emotional lives to the upheaval associated with moving from one country and its language and culture to another.

One day we were working on expressing a fraction as an equivalent fraction with a different denominator. It was the fourth time this year that the students in this group had encountered this topic; the first time was in the fall and the other three times in similar small-group interventions. Each time, we had spent several class sessions, and I had approached the topic in many ways— traditionally and with models of different kinds. And when I brought it up again, their faces were those of deer in headlights.

The students were sure they could not do the math. However, I approached it the way I used to approach playing the same song over and over again when I was in a rock band. It might have been my eleven thousandth time. But for my students, it needed to seem like the first.

I modeled the first one, explaining the logic behind each step I took. Still deer in headlights. I outlined the second one, leaving some blanks in the numbers and the models, and asked questions to ease them into the process. Then the third, the fourth. By the sixth or seventh I was pushing, "Come on! You just did this! You can do it again. Look at the pattern." And by the tenth, I left them alone to solve it together. After almost 20 minutes of direct instruction, I went to tend to a different group.

When I returned 5 minutes later, the deer were gone. Only the light was left. They all had these shifty smiles. They looked as if they had done something naughty. I went over and sat down. "What's going on here?"

"Well, we got it," Monica said.

"What did you get?"

She told me the answer she had, and I asked to see her work. She showed me, still with that glint in her eyes. I said, "It's absolutely correct."

"Well, it's easy."

I chuckled, "Oh, really?"

There were nods all around the table. I said, "Okay, when did *that* happen?"

"When did what happen?"

"When did it get easy?"

They did not know. They thought some sort of magic had taken place. I had to remind them about the first time we discussed the concept months ago, and the many other times since then. I needed to remind them of the looks on their faces when we started just a half hour earlier, and how those looks betrayed how truly uncomfortable they were. It was important to remind them of the journey they had taken to reach this success so that they would be willing to take that journey again and again—so they knew they were strong enough to brave it the next time they needed to.

It turns out it was not as far in the future as one would have thought or hoped. We went on to add and subtract fractions with unlike denominators and it was time to use the skill of finding equivalent fractions. But now it was in a morass of several other needed math skills. And the deer were back. But there were fewer of them. And they were not as scared. And they did not stay as long. Some of them were gently prodding the others with, "Hey, we know how to do this already. Remember?" And most of them did.

A few will likely need to review the skill again in a couple of weeks. Success is not neat and tidy and absolute. But the progress is significant.

Ways Students Build Expertise through Effort

Some classrooms are experimenting with different ways to deliver instruction and content to students. In Woodland Park High School in Colorado, educators Jonathan Bergman and Aaron Sams have "flipped" their classrooms. Instead of delivering instruction in the classroom and sending assignments home with the students, these two teachers post their lectures and instruction online for students to access at home. Then, when students come to class, the teacher and students work together on the assignments in small collaborative groups or in individual sessions that are more akin to coaching (Bergmann and Sams 2011). In a blog post for *The Daily Riff* on January 12, 2011, these high school science teachers noted that "as we roam around the class, we notice the students developing their own collaborative groups. Students are helping each other learn instead of relying on the teacher as the sole disseminator of knowledge. It truly is magical to observe. We are often in awe of how well our students work together and learn from each other."

Think back to some of the coaching examples we have highlighted and picture athletes or musicians working to perfect their skills. Imagine teaching a tennis player how to hit a backhand or a guitar player how to play the major chords by using a short video, a verbal description of the process, and assigning a short passage to read. You then send your young athlete or musician home to practice with a promise of a quiz on their progress when they return the following day. Sounds like a recipe for frustration.

By flipping their classrooms, educators maximize their students' opportunity to engage in expert practice. They make their ground strokes and develop a rhythm in a setting filled with supportive peers and expert coaches. A missed hit or out-of-tune note can be immediately inspected, corrected, and practiced again. Immediate, accurate feedback makes learning tasks even more meaningful, because learners—in the classroom, on the court, and in the studio—can see the fruits of their labors and the influence of subtle changes to their technique.

Resources for Students and Teachers Aspiring to Improve

Mathematics

- Ten Marks© allows students to reinforce mathematical skills.
- Mangahigh.com© offers online mathematics games that target skills that are not typically part of math games (e.g., order of operations, prime numbers, ordering fractions).

Reading and Language Arts

- Many public libraries have books on CDs. Some even have audiobooks preloaded onto MP3 players. Many students already have MP3 players too, and can use a public library to borrow an audiobook to download. Audiobooks can be used to support a student while reading a traditional book.
- ReadWriteThink© was developed by the International Reading Association and National Council of Teachers of English. This site features interactive tools designed for students to help them organize their ideas and participate in activities that teach concepts about language.
- Wordle© makes word clouds from text you enter or copy and paste. A student could copy a whole written piece and paste it into Wordle©, which would then make a pleasing composition of the words.

General

- BrainPOP® has animated movies, supplementary text, and quizzes for students to take in all curricular areas.
- Animoto© is a great option for teachers looking for electronic means for students to show what they know. Instead of writing a report or making a poster, students can make a video using Animoto©.

Thinking and Teaching in 2.0: Building Expertise

Create a table similar to the one shown in Figure 5.2 which lists a selection of skills or strategies students must master to eventually achieve success with higher-level thinking skills. List different skills across content areas and the different ways you have seen students successfully (and not so successfully) master them through practice. We have used revising writing as an example.

Fig. 5.2. Using practice to build successful thinking skills

Skill/ Strategy	How Students Practice	How Successful Are They?	Alternative Idea
Revising writing	Writer's workshop, multiple mini-lessons on revising and dedicated time in class to practice	Somewhat; students depend on teacher for feedback too much	Use Google docs™ and "3 before me" strategy. (Collect 3 comments from classmates first before conferring with teacher)

- Is there a 2.0 tool that would enhance how you address one of these challenges?
- Do you have a mechanism for helping students discover their own methods for developing strategies for enjoyable practice?

Chapter 6

Tools for Authoring, Collaborating, and Organizing Content and Ideas

Ruminations

Two point oh. It is a ubiquitous phrase. We encounter it in television shows and advertisements. When we search our memories, it seems that software writers started this numbering system to help identify and anticipate new versions of their programs. At least once a year, rumors start circulating, promoting the next new smart phone version and the über-hip are are already clamoring for version 6.0 before version 5.0 has even been released.

Still, the term Web 2.0 means something more than "a new version of the Web." In fact, it is a fundamental shift in thinking, in both the medium and how we use the medium. What began as a platform for simply viewing information stored as hypertext is now a rich interface of images, text, links, and applications that invite the user to create and interact with the content. In fact, Rosenblatt's (1969) influential thinking on reading as a two-way transaction between the reader and the text now has an upgrade to consider, the machine behind the cloud. Could it be Rosenblatt 3.0, the transaction between reader, text, and computer applications?

The term *Web 2.0* was used at least as far back as 1999 in an article by Darcy DiNucci who prophetically compared the old web to the new: "The relationship of Web 1.0 to the Web of tomorrow is roughly the equivalence of Pong [one of the earliest computer games that featured a white cube, a pixelated version of a ping-pong ball, that players sent back and forth across the screen] to *The Matrix*." She articulated the paradigm shift in equally eloquent terms: "The Web will be understood not as screenfuls of text and graphics but as a transport mechanism, the ether through which interactivity happens" (DiNucci 1999, 221–222).

As a label, Web 2.0 seems to have become common parlance around 2005 as the Internet shifted from being a repository of information and ideas to the transport mechanism for interactivity that DiNucci described. The Web metamorphosed from a static medium that only provided information to one that allows the user to manipulate the information. It is a jump that radio and television never made; the Web stopped talking at us and allows us to talk back.

Part of the allure of Web 2.0 is the removal of barriers of time, distance, and cost to promote mass collaboration. Open source is another resource often associated with new media and online content development. Open source models allow for many contributors to alter and update content, code, and design. The California Open Source Textbook Project and OER (Open Educational Resources) Commons are two organizations that have tapped into the coordinated power of educators sharing resources and learning. Educators have long been collaborative; the "notion that innovation proceeds through the recombination of existing ideas to form something new is not new to the Web, or even the last century" (Tapscott and Williams 2006, 188). How do we promote the mash-up of the most effective practices and the most promising innovations?

The eyes of a thousand invested educators make for a pretty good source for editing, fact-checking, and troubleshooting.

Mash-up is a term used by web developers to describe the combination of content or data from more than one source into a single site, and by musicians to describe a piece of music created by putting together parts of songs that already exist. It has gained wider usage and can describe any whole made of distinct original parts that have been blended well—from music to visual art to written pieces.

Nowadays, the Web is liberally spattered with content from all walks of life. Information from every continent, in almost every language, and from nearly every point of view can be found. In a quest to get content from every country on Earth, CNN's citizen journalism project, iReport, reached its goal in December 2010 with a post from Nauru, a nation in the South Pacific, prompting the reporter to ask, "How many people would have known about Nauru?" (Hopkins 2010). An article in Wikipedia entitled *Web 2.0*, now mentions a Web 3.0. One wonders what that will be.

Fortunately, using Web 2.0 tools has never been more user-friendly. If you can write and send an email, and are willing to be patient with yourself, you will be able to use a huge number of these tools. And you should. Here is an analogy: We are all reading teachers in one way or another. How effective would you be as a reading teacher, if you did not read? Not very. Regardless of what you teach, you can and should incorporate technology in order to teach more effectively. We are all technology teachers to some extent.

What Is in the Toolbox?

Several types of Web 2.0 tools are available:

- Authoring tools, such as blogs and podcasts
- Collaboration tools, such as wikis and social bookmarking
- Organizational tools, such as tags
- Customization tools, (e.g., extensions) that allow users to personalize their experiences on the Web by changing how their browsers, home pages, and online presence look and function

Again, there is no way to make an exhaustive list of these tools. To do so would be akin to conducting the national census, but rather than trying to do it every ten years, you would start again every ten days. Some days it feels like every ten minutes, as there are more tools popping up each time you open your browser while other tools have met their demise. And the tools themselves often do not fit neatly into categories. For example, bookmarking tools can be organizational in nature because you tag each URL as you save it. If you share them with others, the tools are collaborative as well. Some bookmarking tools even allow you to author slide shows with an image of the homepage of every URL of the bookmarks you are sharing.

As a general rule, it is not too hard to find avid readers on any school staff—just like shooting fish in a barrel. How do we pick what to read? Or, more importantly, how do we pick what not to read? Even the most well-read among us have secret sins of omission (the classics we have never read and are embarrassed to admit so to colleagues and friends). Still, it is impossible to read everything, even when we limit our selection to specific time periods and genres. We "simply have no chance of seeing even most of what exists. Statistically speaking, you will die having missed almost everything" (Holmes 2011). According to blogger Linda Holmes, our options are either to cull our choices or surrender ourselves to the fact that we do not have time to read everything.

Just as media and technology evolve, so must our definitions of what it means to be well-read. Perhaps being well-informed is a better choice; being well-informed is not only more realistic, it also promotes a healthier definition for being inquisitive, open to change, and firmly planted in a growth mindset.

We all have our favorite foods and our favorite sources for recipes and restaurants to enjoy them. Rather than keep track of them everyone, we seek out experts and friends to keep the flow of information manageable. Technology is no different; find someone you trust to help you winnow down the flow of information.

A Tool for Every Season, a Reason for Every Medium

You will find as your use of Web 2.0 tools increases, the high standards you have always set will not change. Clarity in communication, pride of presentation, and accuracy of information will continue to be important—sometimes even more so because students will be aware that in some cases these finished assignments can be viewed by anyone with Internet access.

Just as you vary the media and types of traditional assignments you give, you should vary the types of 2.0 tools you use. Many students spend a great deal of time on the Internet. If school materials and assignments are accessible online, that sometimes offers enough inspiration for students to engage with the content they are trying to learn. In fact, as our students transition from elementary to middle and high school, it will increasingly be their expectation that assignments, reading selections, hyperlinked bibliographies, and online forums for questions and answers are the norm for school coursework, especially in communities that are wired at rates rapidly approaching one hundred percent.

Authoring Tools: Blogs and Vlogs

The word *blog* comes from *weblog,* a merging of the two words *web* and *log.* Teachers can use blogs to communicate with students and their families. Blogs can be used to keep families up to date on what is going on in class as well as to reach out to students and provide help and resources for them once at home. Families can subscribe to a teacher's blog so they are emailed each time something new is posted.

In fact, as blogging tools become increasingly accessible and easy to use, teachers' classroom web pages will more often be in a blog format. The advantages are significant: blogs are editable online from anywhere there is Internet access and do not require special software. Students can use blogs for a variety of assignments. They can use a blog to showcase their writing, keep a reading, learning, or travel journal, express opinions, and display data, information, and conclusions. Many blogs have a feature that allows visitors to comment, which allows classmates to use this Web 2.0 tool to interact regarding academic ideas.

As the price for embedding high quality cameras in computers and handheld devices continues to drop, it becomes increasingly difficult to buy a new computer or mobile phone that does not have a video camera included with the hardware. Video blogging, or *vlogging,* is just what it sounds like. Rather than sharing written information in a blog, a vlog shares information via video.

Authoring Tools: Podcasts and Digital Storytelling

Pod, in the case of *podcast,* is an acronym for 'personal online device.' The *cast* part of the word comes from *broadcast.* So a *podcast* is a broadcast you can listen to or view (then sometimes called a *vodcast*) on a personal online device.

With a podcast, you have an updated version of the radio show. When video is added, it can be a series of still slides or moving video. With the former, you have a narrated slide show and with the latter, a video with sound.

You might have heard the term *digital storytelling*. When used broadly, this refers to any information related by someone using a digital tool. When viewed, its personal nature distinguishes it from professionally produced video and audio. Today's tools help users create finished products that are slick enough to be thrilling for the author—adult or child—and their audience to see, but not corporate slick. It is more personal.

Digital storytelling has many more forms than podcasting. It can run the gamut from using Audacity® to record and manipulate audio, to using the audio as a soundtrack for Blabberize© or VoiceThread©. Students can make digital pop-up books on Zooburst© or amazing videos with Animoto© and Xtranormal©.

Digital Storytelling and Podcast Tools

- Audacity is a free, downloadable tool that lets you record and edit sound.
- Blabberize allows you to choose a photo and manipulate it to make it look like it is talking. You can record the sound in Blabberize or use an MP3 you created with Audacity or some other way.
- VoiceThread is a tool that allows you to create a slide show in which the slides are stills, videos, or documents. However, the slide show is collaborative because people who see it can comment in a variety of ways.
- ZooBurst is a tool that you can use to create 3D-like pop-up books online.

- Animoto is very Apple-flavored in that the video you get when you are done is surprisingly professional looking. There is no way to comment with audio, but you can set your images and video to music. Animoto is very good to educators.

- Xtranormal puts your words in the mouths of animated characters. You have likely seen one on YouTube or as a commercial on television. Xtranormal is also good to educators.

Collaboration Tool: The Wiki

Wikipedia is the most famous wiki. But it is only one of many. The best description either of us has ever seen of a wiki is from Common Craft, *Wikis in Plain English* (2007).

A wiki is a cross between a document and a website. When you click the edit button, it is a document. You can add text, links, and images. You can embed videos. When you are done editing, it is a website. Who can edit? It depends on who has permission. But the other crucial aspect of what makes a wiki a wiki is that it is collaborative. While several people can work on a wiki from disparate locations, it is not uncommon to see hundreds (or even thousands) of users make meaningful contributions to the upkeep of an issue or task-based wiki, especially when time is of the essence. Organizations now drive change through the collaborative efforts of employees, customers, and constituents, a rapid departure from the hierarchical governance much more common in the past century. Rather than information flowing in one direction, from creator to consumer, there are more opportunities to find solutions and share innovations through peer production (Tapscott and Williams 2006).

A Classroon Anecdote: Wikis in Lisa's Classroom

Each year, my students make a social studies wiki using Wikispaces. Instead of filling out organizers on workbook pages, students incorporate facts they find into the wiki. Each page of the wiki is a category of information, and the opening page has instructions and important rules so students understand what is expected of them. Students are responsible for:

1. adding rules when they think of them;

2. reading the facts that other students have already contributed;

3. editing factual and writing mistakes, regardless of who made them; and

4. adding facts of their own.

It is a bit difficult in the beginning for a teacher to read and leave the mistakes—especially the factual ones. But it is quite amazing to see what the group can do as a whole. The process of contributing, and especially of reading what is already there with a critical eye was a deep learning experience for the students involved. They knew their stuff.

Figure 6.1 shows my students' wiki about Ferdinand Magellan. It is an early draft and the mistakes that appear were subsequently edited and revised as the students interacted with one another and with me.

Fig. 6.1. Fifth grade students' wiki about Ferdinand Magellan

> Ferdinand Magellan was born in Portugal but sailed for Spain. He left Spain on September 20, 1519 and when he was crossing the Atlantic Ocean, there were huge storms and fighting on the ship. While they were traveling, one ship was ruined and another one secretly headed back to Spain. It took Magellan thirty-eight days to reach to another ocean and Magellan actually named it the Pacific Ocean and the way to the Pacific Ocean is now called the Straight of Magellan. When he first started sailing, he didn't know it was going to be so horrid and they didn't know they would had such small supplies and soon they ran out, so some men died. On April 27, 1521 Magellan past away in the Philippines by two tribes. Magellan started out with 5 ships but now they only had 2 left because of dangerous circumstances. Hey, did you know the vikings were similar to the Native Americans because they both moved to places to survive?

Organization and Collaboration Tool: Social Bookmarking

It was a relief when browsers started including a way to store, or "bookmark" favorite websites so it was easy to return to them. The downside was that they were stored locally—on the computer one was currently using. So if you were using a different computer, those stored websites were lost.

Social bookmarking services allow you to store the addresses of websites, tag them, and share them with others. Delicious© and Diigo© are examples of such services. Each has its own features, but they both give you the option to make public and private bookmarks and tag bookmarks and share them with others.

Tags

Tags are keywords and are used in many different applications. They are used in social bookmarking services to make the sites you save easier to find later. For example, if you use five or six websites for worksheets, you can label them with the keyword, "worksheet"—otherwise known as tagging. If three of those are great for math worksheets and not much else, they can be tagged with "math" as well.

If teachers want to find those sites the following week or the following year, they can search under the terms "math" and "worksheet" to get the three that are good for math worksheets, or just "worksheet" to see all of your worksheet sites. They can search under just "math" too which might include interactive sites with math games. The more tags the teacher uses, the more specific their results will be.

Tags can be used with blog posts, too. If the educator is a blogger, you can choose the tags that will help the reader find a past blog post on the subject of interest. If the blog post you are writing is about classroom goals in reading, then he or she might give it the tags goals, reading, and summarizing. A year later, if the educator or a student wanted to see what they wrote about classroom goals, they can search the blog using the keyword "goals" and see what comes up. Most blogs have a search function.

Tags are sometimes organized in tag clouds. A cloud in this sense is a collage of words, the ones that are used most often being larger than the rest. The blog Lisa uses at school allows her to display a tag cloud in the margin of the blog so that viewers can see which tags she has used most and least often. The tags for Lisa's blog are shown in Figure 6.2 below. Viewers of her blog can also click on any of the tags to do a search for entries labeled with a particular tag.

Fig. 6.2. Screenshot of tag cloud for Lisa's school blog

Tags

BookOrder conferences Diigo EndOfYear ERR **goals** internet ISATs **math** metecognition ODE questioning **reading** resources SnowDay social_studies technology TenMarks WallWisher WelcomeBack WorkSamples

Bridging Informal and Formal Learning

Are we asking the right question when we query "to blog or not to blog?" As you explore these different tools for learning, expressing, sharing, and interacting, look at your own learning habits. If you want to learn more about the connections between the plasticity of a student's developing brain and the role mirror neurons play in processing the actions of others, what would be the first step you take: library or Internet? The hurdles that had to be previously cleared in order to merely find the information (including gas money to get to the nearest public library for help) are replaced (or in many cases, augmented) by a series of mouse clicks. What is more important now—how to find the information, or how to use information wisely?

As Holmes (2011) shared, if you were just to read the "classics" at a pace of about one hundred books a year, you would be missing out on the vast majority of what has been and will be published. Taking her advice to cull your choices is even more applicable to Web 2.0 tools. What are you interested in? What can you manage? What is realistic?

It is much easier to be open-minded and accepting when the potential weight and volume of the web is not bearing down on you. "Culling," Holmes explains during her report for National Public Radio (April 2011), "implies a huge amount of control and mastery." That is the gift we want to impart to our learners. The formal learning that takes place in the classroom is only the starting point; the informal learnings that classroom lessons inspire are a truer testament to our legacy as educators. There will always be new tools and new media to use, consume, and improve; focus on what you want to learn and achieve. In the 21st century, you can be the producer and director of your own learning, and that is what makes all the difference.

Thinking and Teaching in 2.0: Using the Tools

Authoring. Collaborating. Organizing. Featured in this chapter, these activities are more than strategies to highlight in a 2.0 classroom—they are essential skills that students have always needed. So often, new ideas crowd out old ones, creating an atmosphere of subtraction by addition. Think about meaningful activities and content that are important to your classroom and already in place.

How might any of the tools or concepts featured in this chapter:

- help make the learning objectives for a unit or lesson more accessible to your students?
- encourage students to engage in more authentic, informal learning on their own, extending the ideas you explored in your class?
- help with differentiating instruction?
- enable students to work collaboratively?

Social Networking and Online Presence

Ruminations

April 2011 was an interesting month in the world of digital privacy. When news that the iPhone© created an unencrypted file on your computer that had data about every place your phone—and consequently you—had visited, your response probably fell into one of two camps: the "So what? I already post where I am on Facebook™ anyway" camp, or the camp of moral outrage at the potential invasion of your privacy. This news story gives us a great example of the first level of apprehension for many educators: uncertainty about security, and a general concern for student safety as well as that of teachers.

The applications students used in early computer labs were largely limited to word processing, presentation, and brainstorming programs. Once such programs were installed on your district's computers, all you had to worry about was an occasional upgrade every year or two. Online bulletin boards could keep track of the programs on the market, providing updates and reviews on a regular basis. Consequently, if you were really lucky, when the district offered to spring for a new keyboarding program so your students could learn the home row—you knew which program would give you the best combination of functionality and cost.

Now, as computing begins a migration to wireless handheld devices, the number of available applications, between the Apple® and Android™ platforms alone, is staggering: close to half a million and growing daily (Apple 2011; Oran 2011). In the course of a few short years, we have graduated from a manageable handful of programs, to a menagerie of applications that seems to multiply overnight. During the month it took us to write the first draft of this chapter, the number of applications for the two dominant platforms doubled to half a million. Thus, the second level of apprehension looms: just when you thought it was safe to load that app, you are pulled back in with a newer version that you have to learn before kicking off your next unit in social studies.

To top it all off, do a quick search on this phrase: "teacher fired for Facebook post." The stories are too numerous to count, much less read. Ask any school district's law firm if teachers are held to a higher standard than other professions when it comes to online behavior. The answer is simple and straightforward: Yes. Although many posts that lead to dismissal or disciplinary action are deserving of the consequences, others merely show teachers having a glass of wine with dinner. Even though these stories all happen away from the school day and on personal time, you can bet that every teacher will think twice about any social media crossing their digital classroom door.

So, here we have a trifecta of aggravations: uncertainty about security, more programs than you could possibly choose from, and the potential for personal or professional disaster with a single misstep. What is not to love about the new social media that Web 2.0 can bring into your world and that of your students? Before you run screaming from the room, consider this: What would you do if you knew your children's futures would be influenced, *for better or worse, based on how they managed their digital footprints? To put it another way, how do you prepare your teenager (or more importantly, yourself) for taking those first steps towards learning how to drive? Hide the keys or send them to driver's ed?*

If the first thing college recruiters and potential employers do is an online search when screening today's young adults who have lived through the first wave of social media, what chance do today's middle and high school students have after spending a decade in the online trenches? As educators, we have one question: Do we really want to leave our students' exploration of these new media to chance?

Social Networking

About the same time as the iPhone debacle, AT&T™ and Yahoo's beta email program quietly announced that users' email would be scanned, so companies could offer users new and exciting products they might want to consider buying. Even though users could opt out of this feature, the stake that most Americans have in their privacy is too high to ignore this new reality. This cultural shift moving upon a generation raised on social media and unconcerned with privacy begets a new instructional paradox—how do we save students from their digital selves?

Until recently, conversations about children having it "easier these days" would likely have been quickly dismissed. Not anymore. Even though, as adults, we tend to forget the transgressions of our youth, today's social media will not give the new generation that same luxury. Their actions are permanently stamped in the consciousness of the digital cloud. And, once the "picture" is out there, it is out there for good. There is no way to unring that bell.

Truth has a new ring to it, and it is in the eye (or webcam) of the beholder. And, since many of those beholders will be online when you are not there to defend yourself, the opinion they develop is up for grabs. So, even though educators teach children about all kinds of dangers, are they to leave social networking off limits? Given the stakes, at the very least it would be irresponsible. In an era where online identity has influence on future economic viability, can educators afford to leave it to their students on their own to decipher and figure out how to use social media responsibly?

To understand the importance of how digital behavior and practices influence our lives in the brick and mortar world, it is important to understand how rapidly information-gathering practices on the Web are evolving. Until recently, online searches would produce the same results, regardless of who was searching as long as the search description was identical (Gross 2011). In other words, it used to be that whether it was Susan in Seattle or Raj in Raleigh, if they entered "chocolate chip cookie recipe," they would see the same results. Your digital footprint is no longer limited to what you post on a social networking site anymore; each step your searching, shopping self makes is aggregated to personalize your web experience.

Pariser (2011) highlights this phenomenon with a striking example in his online video clip, "What Is the Internet Hiding from You?" He shares two different screen shots of two different friends searching on the term "Egypt" and displays their results. One returned links to the then-current crisis in Egypt; the other returned suggestions for travel planning. We are making the transition from "you are what you eat" to "you are what you read" to "you are what you click." As you can see, the marketing potential behind what drives the Internet is too big to ignore. In an era where technology has allowed us to bypass commercials on broadcast television, a new way to target and identify audiences has emerged.

As algorithms evolve and are able to target end users by the keyboard taps and mouse clicks they make, the Internet becomes less and less of the great equalizer when it comes to information access. When the goal is to maximize the number of eyeballs on each section of each Web page, the traditional interaction between author, text, and reader gains a fourth wheel—the machinery and the programs that make information flow on the Web possible. It often seems like a race between content developers and algorithm writers; while technical writers and Web page designers use styles to maximize the number of hits on their sites, search engine programmers rush to create smarter and more intuitive heuristics in order to separate the wheat from the chaff of Internet information and content.

So, Big Brother is finally here, and it is not an institution or a government. It is an equation.

Before we go much further, let us look back to the question that got us here in the first place: What role does social networking play in our students' lives and education? Social networking is the most concrete embodiment of the idea "you are what you click." We can use this increasingly familiar vehicle to help students understand how their so-called private lives online really are not that private at all.

Ironically, browsing online may not truly be browsing any longer, as the results we uncover from searches are funneled in ways we may not even realize. In an interview published online in the *Atlantic*, Nicholas Carr (2010) describes "Googlethink—the giant's creepy efforts to read my mind. … every time Google™ presents me with search terms customized to what I'm typing, it reminds me that the company monitors my every move." To put browsing online in context, consider the editorial pages of respected newspapers in the United States which contain columns with opposing views and letters to the editor in support of or in contrast to recently shared opinions. Step into a time machine and go back ten or twenty years when literate and involved people spent time each day reading those pages. Although readers might not agree with the ideas espoused in a percentage of those columns, they might find themselves reading an opposing opinion to better understand the issue from another viewpoint or to test their own arguments. And regardless of agreement or lack thereof, there would be some trust in the quality of the ideas and writing because the writing was edited and vetted by professionals. Also, a professional and cultural filter was present, presumably guided by a code of professional ethics.

While some people still get a print newspaper every day and make an attempt to read viewpoints that differ with their own, online habits are different. Apparently, even if we want to, it will take more considerable effort to seek out those opposing views. Pariser (2011) shares a humorous anecdote in his same talk. In his online network of friends, he organized his contacts into conservative and liberal groups. One day, when he was on his Facebook™ account, he noticed that all of his conservative colleagues no longer appeared in his news feed of daily updates from friends. The social networking software analyzed his clicks and, without his permission, decided he would no longer be interested in the ideas and posts his conservative friends shared.

The code in the machine (or, more likely, in the cloud) is now exhibiting a major step forward in its ability as a reader: it is determining importance for you, the user. Before we look at how this might influence our classroom instruction and our students' intellectual development as students in (and of) the 21st century, let us look back on social networking's development in the early stages of this century and how it influenced how we view the interaction between student, school, and the Internet.

Social Media

Gibby Miller launched what is thought to be the first widely used social networking site in 2000 (Wappler 2008). In an era where social networking sites measured growth of their sites' popularity by tracking the number of new and active visitors in the tens and hundreds of millions, Miller's site tracks visitors in the thousands.

What is interesting, is the name of this site, Makeoutclub™. This domain name epitomizes some of the early leeriness educators and adults had as young adults flocked to these applications in droves. As one colleague shared following a law firm's session on the potential perils students and teachers face when using social networking sites inappropriately, "No one over thirty-five has any business being on one of these sites." At the very least, it is a twist on the adage from the sixties, "trust no one over thirty."

As social networking exploded as an application through the first decade of the new millennium, sites such as Friendster™, MySpace™, and Facebook rode the wave of enthusiasm for this symbol of interactivity on the newest frontier of the Internet. The image launched by Makeoutclub™ continued to dominate social networking, as these sites were associated with college and high school students posting pictures of parties and alcohol-fueled high jinks for the whole world to see. But, as 2000's first decade came to a close, analysis of Facebook traffic (the dominant social networking site at the time) by iStrategyLabs (2011) indicated a graying of Facebook users, as growth in the percentage of users over 25 far outpaced the growth of 18–24 year-old users (Schroeder 2009).

How cool can social networking be if your parents (and grandparents) use it, too? As with any new tool, when use by trendsetters transitions to general use by the public, efficacy and acceptable use become increasingly the norm.

While writing this book, we accessed social networking groups and applications that included:

- Pages maintained by individuals, such as cognitive psychologist Daniel Willingham's Facebook page, which included his thoughts, reactions to articles and events, and links to prominent thinking in the field of student motivation and neuroscience.

- Pages maintained by groups of individuals, such as an online community moderated by publisher Jason Low of Lee & Low Books, where he invited colleagues in book publishing, educators, authors, illustrators, and experts from other related fields to discuss trends in all fields related to publishing and writing for children and young adults.

- Sites maintained by organizations, such as the Engage community developed by the International Reading Association, to provide educators and literacy professionals with a social networking and resource area to discuss current trends in reading research and instruction.

- Goodreads©, a site that has similar features to that of Facebook™, but all based on books users have read.

We can imagine a new marketing campaign, "Social networking. It's not just for your preteen anymore." Still, the main challenge is figuring out how to manage the quality of the time we spend reading and learning in this medium. Perhaps this tool will become so commonplace that its novelty wears off and its use becomes as commonplace as word processing, pencil, and paper; perhaps it will continue to be a medium that favors frivolity. In any case, it is a tool that warrants the attention of educators.

Collaboration in a 2.0 World

Transitioning into the world of social networking can often begin out of necessity. Sometimes, the only way to access a specific person's or group's ideas is through the platform they chose to promote the discussion. In one such group, a conversation about e-publishing took on a life of its own. As writers, publishers, educators, and technology experts from around the United States and Canada joined in to share perspectives, it was clear that without this technology, accessing this wide range of expertise and insight would have been nearly impossible, simply due to geography and personal schedules. Yet, here we were, with teachers, poets, and business people alike, working together to explore a challenge centered on a specific theme.

In a nutshell, that is the allure of social networking. It allows you to build groups for particular purposes by removing the barriers of time and distance that so often block effective communication and collaboration. While we still might have hurdles to overcome with deciding on what common tools to use and their respective learning curves, there still are some basic tenets we can work on to make the experiences accessible for our professional selves and for our students' experiences in and out of the classroom. We will use two lenses to focus, one on process (collaboration) and one on content (independent reading).

Taking part in or joining a social networking group involves making a commitment to a common interest or cause. What starts out as a conversation can lead to a movement, as traditional barriers to sharing information dissipate online. Understanding a framework for the different levels of engagement possible can make working together on framing curriculum and instruction or developing authentic purposes for units of study more productive. This model for collaboration in a Web 2.0 world, as shown in Figure 7.1, is adapted from Clay Shirky's work in *Here Comes Everybody: The Power of Organizing without Organization* (2008, 47–54).

Fig. 7.1. Collaboration model for Web 2.0 world

Level 1: Sharing	• Knowingly sharing your work with a group
	• Few guidelines or limitations; the goal is simply to distribute information based on a specific theme
	• Maximum freedom for individual members
	• Example: photo sharing site, where all rights are released

Level 2: Cooperation	• Membership in a group with a shared interest or goal • Changes in individual behavior to promote fitting in with group identity • Example: Online discussion group focusing on the role e-books play in the future of writing, publishing, and purchasing books
Level 3: Collaborative Production	• More involved form of cooperation • Increasing tension between individual members and group goals, as consensus must be reached • Participation of all group members is necessary for success; no one member can take credit over another • Example: Wiki document, where shared authorship is necessary to maintain accuracy
Level 4: Collective Action	• Usually involves largest membership • Action is taken in the name of a group • Individual members may have to sacrifice needs or wants, even to their individual detriment, for group action to succeed • Example: Rationing by a community; although you may be hungrier, everyone survives

A Classroom Anecdote: Using Goodreads® and Wikispaces to Promote Independent Reading

In building a community of readers in my classroom, I thought about how my reading friends and I shared book recommendations. We talked about books we read, created book clubs, and sought opinions. I wondered about how to mirror

that in my classroom. _____
available, we used a lo_____
for writing book recomm_____
We had a "What We _____
which everyone posted _____
name of the book they we_____
seemed to enjoy looking _____
completed the book recor_____
were assigned.

Eventually we found _____
Internet access, both at sc_____
the last few years, the perc_____
my fifth grade classroom wit_____
been at or near 100%. So, c_____
Goodreads©. I had joined, _____
students about it (and their _____ anyone
under 13 needed parental permission), I joined
a second time as the teacher version of myself.
I locked down my personal account and left my
teacher persona account as public.

At first, two or three students joined. I
recommended books to them, and they to me. I
actually read the books they recommended and
posted opinions and ratings. They followed suit.
Eventually, approximately 20 current and former
students were in an online community posting
book reviews, recommending books, and posting
written pieces, too.

Two years after starting with Goodreads, I
learned about Wikispaces. I began using it with
students so that they could curate information
about the topics we were studying in social
studies. The wiki turned out well, but had an
unforeseen consequence: students began starting
their own wikis. One wiki was a student's answer
to Goodreads. Jasmine created a beautiful wiki
that provided a space for her and her friends to
discuss and debate books they were reading. Later

ar, she and her classmates used the wiki
cuss the books in the "Battle of the Books"
petition and subsequently accompanied me to
a district board of education meeting to show what
she had been doing.

Between Wikispaces and Goodreads, my
students did more discussing of books on their
own, of their own volition, than I ever imagined
was possible.

Caught Between the Peril and the Promise

Watching our students share authentic reflections and
recommendations with enthusiasm convinces us of the promise
social networking can provide when wielded responsibly and
purposefully. Watching an undergrad lose his certification to teach
before he even steps into the classroom because of a drunken
pirate photo and accompanying comment gives us pause. Is it
because of the novelty implicit in so many 2.0 frontiers, or is it
because we are just now developing standards of conduct that can
be taught, learned, and applied by our students?

So much of the Web is anonymous, with user names that give
no indication to identity, age, or location. Free speech is certainly
an important tenet and a foundation of our society. It is a right that
we afford to each and every member of society. The question is: Is
the online persona "dangerkitty0u812" perceived of as deserving
the same rights and protections as MaryJane Adams from Hope,
Arizona? An intriguing question to explore and debate, no doubt,
but when it comes to curriculum and classroom application, the
answer probably will not help us.

We want to tap into the promise that social media can
provide. As you explore its potential for instruction, consider these
guidelines:

- Know school district rules and community expectations. As social networking sites are often blocked and filtered, consider a trial project. Rather than focus on social networking as the primary tool, focus on a theme to investigate or content to learn.

- Set standards for posting and explicitly teach online expectations. Do not assume students or parents understand these expectations. Before going online, have students communicate their understanding through an assignment.

- Make sure student usernames are clearly recognizable and identify who the student is. Teach students the importance of password integrity and use closed groups where teachers control who is invited in to participate.

- Communicate the scope of the project with parents and use permission slips to confirm parent understanding of what new media will be used. Use this as an opportunity to share information about online safety and sensible use of social media.

- Make plans for your students who do not have access to an online computer at home. Access is only equitable if everyone has the same opportunity.

Common Sense Media, a non-profit group dedicated to informing parents and educators about surviving a world filled with technology and media, is a good starting point for building connections between school, home, and conversations about the role social media plays in students' lives. Their approach is realistic, focusing on "media sanity, not censorship" (Common Sense Media 2011). With around seventy percent of the web-browsing population of the United States on Facebook as of April of 2011, teaching sanity seems like a good idea (iStrategy Labs 2011).

Thinking and Teaching in 2.0: Social Networking in Practice

Edmodo promotes itself as a "secure social learning network for teachers and students." You have long been curious about how to use a social networking platform for your fourth grade students. As you begin thinking about your unit on the different regions of the United States, it dawns on you that a social learning network would be a great way for students to share what they learn about different regions and a way to connect with a colleague's classroom in another region.

- What challenges do you foresee facing when presenting this idea to your teammates? To your principal? To your students' parents?
- How will you address those challenges?

Chapter 8

Technology Is Not an Event

Ruminations

On Jerry's last big family road trip, he threw caution to the wind, or more accurately, he threw the maps out the window. Armed with a smart phone and a general sense of direction (aided by the compass on the smart phone) he set out for Williamsburg, Virginia. Practicing safe driving techniques, he turned the phone over to his 10-year-old daughter who monitored the turn-by-turn directions and selected side trips with a little input from a couple of travel applications, all the while maintaining that he was not nearly smart enough to use the smart phone. He explained that part of smart driving was not using the smart phone while doing so. He found restaurants that were open and off the beaten path, as well as the best deals on hotels in Columbus, Ohio, and truly felt he had graduated from printing out online directions.

It almost makes an atlas seem arcane. Until, that is, you have thrown out your maps and experience some fabulously inefficient directions from whatever mobile mapping services you have chosen. In exasperation, you wonder why you ditched the atlas. This is where mindset—especially a mindset raised on technology—demonstrates that the medium is not the most crucial element to finding your way, rather it is the flexibility of your thinking that makes all the difference. When a device gave directions that did not make sense, there were two different reactions in our car: 1) reload the *map, maybe even with a different app, or 2) proclaim that it was not a smart phone, but a stupid one, and demand the trusty paper map.*

The point here, though, is not to demean the tool or to indicate which one is better. Making an informed decision is the point. The atlas works best when the app plots an illogical route or your coverage drops; and unlike the map, the mobile application can tell you about traffic and is a whole lot easier to stow. Teaching and learning in the 21st century is mostly about deciding how to access the information, determining the quality of the information you uncover, and having a plan (and direction) for using what you learn. It has much less to do with the tool you use to get it.

In fact, asking what technology to use might not even be the right question. Based on how and when it is asked in the planning process, chances are it could be a disastrously wrong question. "Most educators agree that we need 21st century schools and that we need to prepare students for the information economy. However, what does this really mean, and what are the essential questions and planning processes needed to prepare our students to have a global work ethic?" (November 2010).

Form and Function in Today's World

If you write a lot, the implement you prefer can be inferred by your maladies—pen callus on your finger or carpal tunnel in your wrists. Chances are, though, if you have either of those conditions, you intimately understand the tool that caused them. Practice may make perfect, and practice certainly leaves its mark, whether you like it or not. If you can pardon the pun, here is the rub; when we think about how to effectively learn, do we take more comfort in our calluses or are we willing to chance carpal tunnel?

Most human beings are creatures of habit. Remember, our brains are built to recognize and use patterns, not break them. We stick with the tried and true—sometimes just with the tried. It is certainly important to avoid jumping on the latest bandwagon so that we do not find ourselves on a joyride that takes us far from our intended destination. And there is wisdom in the saying, "If it ain't broke, don't fix it." But our comfortable ain't-broke solutions are not always the best fit for the problems we are trying to address. For example, Lisa had a state-of-the-art overhead projector. Everything she showed on it was clear, bright, and visible to all students in the room. Of course, what she showed was on plastic transparencies. And those transparencies needed plastic sheet protectors in order to organize them and store them for use year after year. And if what she wanted to show was on paper, she needed to copy the image from the paper onto transparencies. And the transparencies needed to be a particular type or they melted in the copier.

Her overhead projector was not broken nor was its method of displaying images and text inadequate. But the document camera she uses now is a better solution. It is greener, it is quicker, and the display is just as clear, bright, and visible. No more filling up landfills with transparencies that will last to the next millennium.

What does it take for someone to be willing to break a habit and try something new? Sometimes discomfort does it in various forms: frustration because something really is broken, indirect peer-pressure because no one is using the ditto maker any longer and you feel as archaic as the machine, or top-down mandates. Check your mindset when you find yourself in this situation; it does not need to be as a result of a negative experience. Perhaps you would like to rethink a lesson or reimagine a unit. You might want to reinvigorate your approach and resuscitate the curriculum so it lives and breathes 21st century air. You may feel like it is time to reinvent yourself as a professional educator and revamp your philosophy of education. Take a step or two outside your comfort zone! Exceed the limits of your programming. Rebuild and reboot.

Just in case you were not yet revulsed by our subtle prefix use, we hope you use the ideas in this book to revisit how you teach and how you will teach.

Although we have spent seven chapters sharing ideas about neuroscience, new media, and technology for a golden age of learning, perhaps you are thinking that finding ways to integrate new media and technology into different units of study is not the way to go. We do not want you to feel that this book is like one of those novels where the likable heroine gets killed off in the end when you were hoping for the happily ever after. Nor do we want to leave you with pie-in-the-sky impossibilities. We do want you to go for a bigger piece of the pie, though. For a starter, find a piece you can have in your classroom, and still keep an eye on the one in the sky for another day. To get a better feel for what we mean, tackle the scenario described in the Weblandia School District 2.0 laptop initiative below.

In Weblandia Elementary School District 2.0, an initiative to put laptop computers in the hands of every child is gaining traction at the school board level. The small school district sits on the banks of the Columbia River and is near the site of a new server farm set up by the upstart tech company, Cloud Computing. Two prominent members of the school board are associated with Cloud Computing, and they are very excited about a one-laptop-per-child initiative.

After some debate, the school district decides to start with a pilot program with its fifth graders at three of the schools. The purchase is approved at a June board meeting and the project is fast tracked to start in the fall, with much excitement brewing in the community. The laptops are prepared and ready to go at the start of the school year, although delivery issues limited teacher training to two half-day workshops the week before school started. The workshops focused on troubleshooting issues with the laptops and an introduction to the free open source productivity suite that came loaded on the system.

The school's wireless network allows for good connectivity throughout the day, even during peak usage times. Through a one-year grant, Weblandia has an on-site technology assistant who splits her time between the three schools and can help with software and hardware issues. The district has not identified a funding source for year two of the initiative. After three months with the laptops, faculty from Weblandia Central Elementary is due to make their first presentation to the board on the progress of this program while focusing on the following questions:

- What successes do you think teachers, students, and families will report?
- What challenges do you think each group will encounter?
- What do you think the follow-up steps will be after the initial phase of implementation?

As with any well-intentioned school initiative, there are components to celebrate and challenges to address. The pluses could include the portability of laptops and the accessibility they provide, a strong network to support increased access, on-site tech support, and a thoughtful plan to pilot the program before extending it to the entire district. The challenges to address, though, are major ones and not uncommon in any school initiative, even those not involving technology. Although there is tech support, what happens in year two when the support fades away and the program presumably expands to more grades, creating more users and more questions? Even bigger, how will teachers be supported in a consistent way so that students have similar experiences and opportunities to grow? Although there is no cost for the software, what is the cost to students if teachers do not have significant (and ongoing) professional development support in the following areas:

- How to use various software applications and online tools to teach each content area

- Guidelines for developing curriculum with technology in mind
- Strategies for using available tools to help differentiate students' experiences
- Access to and input into a district and school curriculum map that outlines goals for 21st century skills and strategies

Without significant time and effort dedicated to teacher and curriculum development, participants are bound to find themselves struggling with any initiative. Although grants and funding sources sometimes come with a "use it or lose it" timeline, getting new tools without an investment in curriculum planning is not just putting the cart before the horse, it is taking the cart and leaving the horse behind. Whether it is a large scale plan such as one-to-one computing, or something as small as trying out a social learning network in your classroom for a single unit, it is crucial to put as much effort into planning the purpose as learning the tool. Excellent planning resources are available from such organizations as the International Society for Technology in Education (ISTE), Northwest Educational Technology Consortium (NETC), and the Partnership for 21st Century Skills (P21). When undertaking an initiative that involves integration of new media or technology, you may find the suggestions in Figure 8.1 to be helpful.

Fig. 8.1. Realistic technology integration for students and teachers

- Provides a clear connection to curriculum
- Enhances 21st century skills: critical thinking, collaboration, communication, creativity
- Plans for timely support with technical hardware and network expertise
- Plans for timely support with technical software and application expertise
- Provides opportunities for greater student engagement and deeper understanding of curriculum learning objectives
- Establishes a timeline for teacher evaluation of program effectiveness
- Supports a school and district administration

In the introduction to *Can You Hear Me Now? Applying Brain Research and Technology to Engage Today's Students*, we opined that we are entering the golden age of learning, a perfect confluence of neuroscience, cognitive psychology, and opportunities afforded by what November (2010) describes as the "most powerful information media ever invented by society" (276). As educators plan for student learning and their teaching, they must each do all they can to keep their practices informed yet avoid being overwhelmed. In short, while students work on wikis and begin to blog, they must have enough time and space to make certain they are learning to be digitally literate.

This golden age of learning will not happen simply because of the presence of technology and information media. In some cases, it may be happening in spite of the resources afforded to our students. Homework or Facebook? Collaboration or chatting? Research or plagiarism? Learners of all ages have always had the potential to be distracted to the point of inefficiency, but now we have more tools than ever to facilitate that condition.

Web 2.0 tools may lower the barriers and increase the equity in education by providing access to a wider range of resources to all learners, but with the lowering of these barriers comes an increase in the responsibility to educate students in the ethics, organization, and focus needed to learn in this hyper-linked, marketing-saturated medium. In our drive to differentiate and optimize learning for each individual student and have all students become more intrinsically motivated and self-directed in their learning, we have the potential to release them too soon into this brave new world. Imagine how the teachers at Weblandia School District 2.0 felt trying to learn new applications and technology with only cursory introductory lessons. How well would your students learn if they were feeling the same way?

Students can still learn how to read, whether it is a real or virtual binding. And, just as combining different forms of information in a new way for better understanding is not the sole province of the 21st century, neither are critical thinking and higher-order thinking skills. To prepare students to compete in a global society, new literacies are to be learned. Since the rules, mores, and ways to interact online and through other media are developing and changing in ways faster than we can predict (and develop curriculum), it would behoove us to put greater emphasis on critical thinking and analysis to prepare our students for the rapid-fire changes they are certain to encounter in their academic, personal, and professional lives.

Sometimes students take things for granted. The way the Web is developing as a marketing engine might work against them. Just as we weave in comprehension strategy instruction in meaningful, authentic ways through our literacy block, learning to read online will take the same integration of strategies through authentic assignments. Curious as to just how much critical thinking your students do while searching online? Take the quiz shown in Figure 8.2 for a test drive with your colleagues first, then with students. Comparing the results might be equally informing and amusing.

Fig. 8.2. How tech-savvy are you?

Directions: Consider how much critical thinking you do while searching and using online resources. For each statement, indicate *true, false*, or *it depends*. Add comments that explain your choice of response.

Statement	true	false	it depends
1. Using one search engine will bring you all the results you need for good research.			
2. The most relevant responses to a query are always on the first page of links provided.			
3. Information published online is factual and verified by experts.			
4. It does not matter who you are or where you search from when you are browsing, the same answers will be provided to any question.			
5. When searching for information, you should not change how you phrase your query; the placement of the words in your query does not influence the search.			
6. There are virtual spiders in the Internet that help browsers find important pages more quickly.			

Bonus Question: How do search engines work? In other words, how can my browser find Web pages about Tahiti in a matter of seconds?

In case you were wondering, the only statement that deserves an answer of true is number 6. There are spiders in the Internet; these little programs search the Web and help create the indexes your browser accesses to find information so quickly, efficiently, and with all the algorithms needed to target the user with appropriate marketing. The way we store and share information is changing fundamentally; with this type of change, fundamental shifts in how we access and consume information are also taking place. We are moving from a static technology (paper) to a dynamic (digital) one (November 2010).

When our written history and information processing was dominated by paper, access was controlled by how you could get to the information (transportation) or how the information could get to you (public or private organizations; bookstores, schools, libraries, etc.). This access could be limited by economics, politics, or logistics. With the transition to a more dynamic, interactive medium, it is much easier to share information that is both worthwhile (cancer research), timely (updates on storm damage to a community), and neither important nor worthwhile (cute kitten videos).

In focusing on the big picture benefits and possibilities, for the first time in history, we may be able to stand on the shoulders of all those that have come before us, not just a select few. Perhaps we can start building on the strengths and contributions of all cultures and communities, rather than just a few of the dominant ones. We are at a digital crossroads, though, because the Web is not designed to promote tolerance, it is designed to steer you towards those who are similar in temperament and mindset to you. So how—with this potent tool—can we ensure that students grow up well-rounded and exposed to a multitude of experiences in order to be more fully informed and analytical?

We teach them. Schools need to continue their mission of helping students grow up thoughtfully, accepting of others, and willing to work collaboratively to solve problems. We teach them that caring begins in the community and grows as a person becomes a global citizen. We learn locally so we can act globally. How do we go about this mission in the 21st century? By looking for junctions between the tasks students must traditionally undertake to grow as learners and making sure that, when possible, they get the chance to use the tools that will be part of their futures. Examples of these skills and technology resources are shown in Figure 8.3.

Figure 8.3. Learning skills and related digital tools and techniques

Learning Skill	Explanation	Digital Tools and Techniques
Finding and analyzing information	Whether researching butterflies or child labor, students will need to be able to determine the quality of the information they are seeing. As content is increasingly stylized and personalized, it will become critical that students are able to ferret out this century's snake oil, no matter how pretty it looks on the Web.	Understanding how browsers work, and the importance of having a diversity of searching techniques and search engines.
Organizing ideas and coordinating resources	No matter how beautiful the prose, a video of cascading monarch butterflies reaching their migration destination of Michoacan, Mexico is probably far more dramatic and memorable. Finding information is not enough; determining the best ways to organize and share important ideas and concepts is crucial in an increasingly connected world.	Using a wiki and social bookmarking tools to collect information from a variety of sources and media, share notes and ideas on how to manage that information, and brainstorm ways to best share what has been learned.

Figure 8.3. Learning skills and related digital tools and techniques *(cont.)*

Learning Skill	Explanation	Digital Tools and Techniques
Building collaborative teams	Finding both experts and interested partners around specific themes, ideas, or issues is facilitated by removing distance barriers.	Use a combination of social learning networks and distance communication tools such as Skype to promote pen-pal projects with classrooms that are in other regions of the country or world.
Creating content	The Web is a visual medium and affords students and teachers many options to make sure that the medium suits the message.	Promote student choice by having multiple options for sharing content by creating videos, podcasts, presentations, or infographics using any of the applications listed in Appendix B. Use rubrics that help students reflect on how effective the medium was for the message they were trying to communicate.
Communicating deeper understanding	Finding meaningful ways to practice and have repeated exposure to key concepts, vocabulary, and content is a way to promote deeper understanding with students. By making them the producers of this content, other students can benefit from their developing expertise.	Short podcasts and videos can be great tools for promoting study habits and solutions to challenging work.

Figure 8.3. Learning skills and related digital tools and techniques *(cont.)*

Learning Skill	Explanation	Digital Tools and Techniques
Sharing opinions	If the key to deeper engagement and greater student motivation is giving them voice and choice in how they share their understanding, then the 21st century is the platform for launching student learning.	Encourage student blogging and classroom social learning networks. To help lessen the burden on teachers, promote use of these tools as a way to explore independent reading, writing workshop extensions, reactions to current events, and homework collaboration.

Allowing students to enter a post-academic world without having a handle on these thinking and learning skills and strategies would be educational malpractice. Although we spent some time as positive deviants at the beginning of this chapter trying to dissuade you from buying into technology trends whole hog, the examples above speak volumes as to why technology can no longer be an event in today's classrooms. Building a new school? Think carefully about creating a computer lab on the blueprint. Do not bring the content or the students to the lab, bring the appropriate technology to the content so it is more accessible, presentable, consumable, or simply more current. Sometimes the best technology is a book, other times it might be an e-reader. A pen or pencil can be more useful than a laptop in certain situations (like when your battery is running low).

The big-picture goal should not be teaching students about each tool and how it works; the prime directive of education must be to show students the wide, wonderful world and make sure they have the ability to engage fully and intelligently with it.

Keep Listening, Exploring, and Learning

As happens with traditional books that are held in a reader's hands, the thickness of this book in your left hand far out-spans that in your right, indicating the impending end. But it feels almost disingenuous to call this the end, given the topics and messages of this book. So, the paper pages may be running out, but for its authors, this book is a conglomeration of ongoing ideas.

We are looking to the future in the way parents hope for and wonder about the future of a child; we are responsible for the memes of this creation, but thanks to scientists and researchers such as David Shenk, we know that the environment will have a huge impact.

Please be a part of that impact. As ideas occur to you, be in touch. You can find us on Twitter and our blog, Born to Be Wired. Let us know what you have tried. Share your experiences and opinions, your voice, and your choices. Thanks to technology, we can hear you now.

Thinking and Teaching in 2.0: Rethink, Revamp, and Regenerate

Form and function matter in today's world. Email carries more weight than text messages; letters are more official than an email. Understanding content may help students develop intellect; understanding the vast array of tools and media develops their ability to better communicate that intellect. If you are willing to experiment, take any successful lesson you have done in the past. Before introducing the lesson and its objectives to this year's students, consider new media or technology that students could use in the process of learning or as a way to create a product that communicates their learning. Then, involve your students in this experiment: randomly split your class into two groups, one to follow your original plan, the other to follow the updated plan. Provide your students with the opportunity to share both their learning and how the medium(s) they used influenced their learning. Slightly alter the task and switch the groups, so both can experience each opportunity.

- What did you learn from the process?
- What did you learn from your students?

Appendix A

Resources for Further Viewing, Reading, and Ruminations

Neuroscience and Cognitive Psychology

Coyle, D. 2009. *The talent code: Greatness isn't born. It's grown. Here's how*. New York: Bantam.

> Daniel Coyle is a great storyteller with an understated sense of humor who seems to have distilled what it takes to create greatness. One of the most wonderful aspects of this book is that people who are successful with children—parents, teachers, administrators—will find the ideas supportive of what they already know.

Dehaene, S. 2009. *Reading in the brain: The science and evolution of a human invention*. New York: Viking.

> The book by Dehaene is worth reading just to appreciate the concept of neuronal recycling. From the work of this author, you can create your own dramatic production entitled, "All You Ever Wanted to Know about How the Brain Learns to Read but were Afraid to Ask." From linguistics and language to neurons, nature, and nurture, these two seminal works should be on every educator's bookshelf.

Doidge, N. 2007. *The brain that changes itself: Stories of personal triumph from the frontiers of brain science*. New York: Viking Penguin.

> This book started us on our pursuit of trying to know all a layperson could possibly know about neuroscience. The stories in this book stunned us, and changed our understanding of the brain, teaching, and learning.

Dweck, C. S. 2006. *Mindset: The new psychology of success*. New York: Random House.

>This book is a great candidate for professional learning communities and teacher book clubs. Perhaps no single idea can help transform school and classroom culture than switching from a *fixed* to a *growth* mindset. Solid research makes this message even stronger. You might also be interested in checking out the Mindset website: http://www.mindsetonline.com.

Pink, D. 2006. *A whole new mind: Why right-brainers will rule the future*. New York: Riverhead.

>Daniel Pink makes the case that the future belongs to those of us with what are traditionally considered right-brained abilities. Abilities to design and play, for example, are ones that computers do not have. Artificial intelligence is not even close to being able to simulate these right-brained abilities, and Pink's claim that those of us who possess them have a better chance at success and satisfaction.

Ramachandran, V. S. 2011. *The tell-tale brain: A neuroscientist's quest for what makes us human*. New York: W. W. Norton & Company.

>We first encountered Dr. Ramachandran in an article in *Scientific American* about a tantalizing concept: mirror neurons. He has an amazing aptitude for designing simple, elegant experiments that reveal breathtaking insights into how our tangled mass of neurons works. One of the most talented neuroscientists writing today, this is his latest work.

Ravitch, D. 2010. *The death and life of the great American school system: How testing and choice are undermining education*. New York: Basic Books.

>Thank goodness for Diane Ravitch's sanity and sense of history. She shines a light in the dark places where poor decisions are being made about education so that you can see clearly what happened and how.

Reeves, D. B. 2003. *High performance in high poverty schools: 90/90/90 and beyond*. Denver: Center for Performance Assessment.

>As unrealistic as it is to put the entire onus for student success or failure on teachers, this article does a wonderful job of taking a positive look at how teachers and administrators can make changes in order to successfully face the challenges of educating at-risk students.

Shenk, D. 2010. *The genius in all of us: Why everything you've been told about genetics, talent, and IQ is wrong*. New York: Doubleday.

>Shenk's ideas are simply inspiring. Read his work to breathe new life into your beliefs that all children can succeed given the right conditions. The reader-friendly work provides a layperson's look at gene expression and offers huge potential for how we think about learning, teaching, and helping all children grow as learners.

Willingham, D. T. 2009. *Why don't students like school? A cognitive scientist answers questions about how the mind works and what it means for the classroom*. San Francisco: John Wiley & Sons.

>Well, the title annoyed us a little, but the book certainly did not. Willingham walks the walk in the writing of this book. Each chapter is centered on a cognitive principle, and each principle is grounded in solid research.

Wolf, M. 2007. *Proust and the squid: The story and science of the reading brain*. New York: Harper.

>The book by Wolf is worth reading just to appreciate the concept of neuronal recycling. From the work of this author, you can create your own dramatic production entitled, "All You Ever Wanted to Know about How the Brain Learns to Read but were Afraid to Ask." From linguistics and language to neurons, nature, and nurture, these two seminal works should be on every educator's bookshelf.

New Media and Technology in Society

Bellanca, J., and R. Brandt (eds). 2010. *21st century skills: Rethinking how students learn.* Bloomington, IN: Solution Tree Press.

> This edited volume provides a compendium of philosophy and frameworks for how educators can start thinking about and integrating new media, technology, and 21st century strategies and skills into their everyday lessons.

Carr, N.. 2008. *The big switch: Rewiring the world, from Edison to Google*. New York: W. W. Norton & Company.

> From the author who wrote "Is Google Making Us Stupid?" in *The Atlantic* (2008, July/August), this book may not have direct classroom application, but it will certainly get you thinking about the ubiquitous search engine and how the nature of computing is changing from local to global. If we continue to follow the path he lays out in this book, in the future you will say, "I remember when we had to carry around our data and programs on a laptop computer."

Shirky, C. 2008. *Here comes everybody: The power of organizing without organization*. New York: Penguin.

> Another book that may not have direct implications for how you teach, but it will certainly leave you with a greater appreciation of how the nature of the Web and online society are changing to a more social, interactive model. If you have an interest in the power and potential of open source and social networking, this book holds many foundational ideas.

List of Websites and Tools

Common Craft's *Wikis in Plain English:* http://www.commoncraft.com/video-wikis-plain-english

Karl Fisch's *Did You Know* **YouTube:** http://www.youtube.com/watch?v=ljbI-363A2Q

Medieval Helpdesk with English subtitles **YouTube:** http://www.youtube.com/watch?v=pQHX-SjgQvQ

Web Tools

Animoto: http://animoto.com/

Audacity: http://audacity.sourceforge.net/

backchan.nl: http://backchan.nl/

Blabberize: http://blabberize.com/

Brainhoney: http://brainhoney.com/

BrainPOP: http://www.brainpop.com/

Delicious: http://www.delicious.com/

Digg: http://digg.com/

Diigo: http://www.diigo.com/

Edmodo: http://www.edmodo.com/home

Free Technology for Teachers: http://www.freetech4teachers.com/

Gliffy: http://www.gliffy.com/

Goodreads: http://www.goodreads.com/

Google Docs: http://docs.google.com/

Google Talk: http://www.google.com/talk/

Mangahigh.com: http://www.mangahigh.com/

Mind42.com: http://www.mind42.com/portal/index.xhtml

Moodle: http://moodle.org/

ReadWriteThink: http://www.readwritethink.org/
classroom-resources/student-interactives/

Skype: http://www.skype.com/

Ten Marks: http://www.tenmarks.com/

TodaysMeet: http://todaysmeet.com/

Udemy: http://www.udemy.com/

VoiceThread: http://voicethread.com/

Wallwisher: http://www.wallwisher.com/

Wiggio: http://wiggio.com/

Wikispaces: http://www.wikispaces.com/

Wordle: http://www.wordle.net/

Xtranormal: http://www.xtranormal.com/

ZooBurst: http://www.zooburst.com/

Rubrics

ReadWriteThink.org: http://www.readwritethink.org

Rubistar4teachers.org: http://rubistar.4teachers.org

http://www.rubistar.4teachers.com/middleschool.php

http://www.rubristar.4teachers.com/languagearts.php

Kathy Schrock's Guide to Assessment and Rubrics: http://
schooldiscoveryeducation.org/schrockguide/assess.html

Teach-nology: http://www.teach-nology.com/web_tools/
rubrics

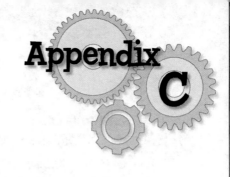

Appendix C

References Cited

Apple. *Apple*. June 2011. www.apple.com/iphone/apps-for-iphone/ (accessed June 20, 2011).

Baccellieri, P. 2010. *Professional learning communities: Using data in decision-making to improve student learning*. Huntington Beach, CA: Shell Education.

Bauerlein, M. 2009. *The dumbest generation: How the digital age stupefies young Americans and jeopardizes our future*. New York: Penguin.

Bean, T. 2010. *Multimodal learning for the 21st century adolescent*. Huntington Beach, CA: Shell Education.

Bergmann, J., and A. Sams. 2011. How the flipped classroom is radically transforming learning. *The Daily Riff.* (January 12) http://www.thedailyriff.com/articles/how-the-flipped-classroom-is-radically-transforming-learning-536.php (accessed May 5, 2011).

Blackmore, S. July 2008. *Susan Blackmore on memes and temes*. http://www.ted.com/talks/lang/eng/susan_blackmore_on_memes_and_temes.html (accessed November 19, 2010).

Bounds, G. October 5, 2010. How handwriting trains the brain: Forming letters is the key to learning, memory, ideas. *The Wall Street Journal*. http://online.wsj.com/article/SB10001424052748704631504575531932754922518.html (accessed November 27, 2011)

Bushaw, W., and S. Lopez. 2010. A time for change: The 42nd annual Phi Delta Kappa/Gallup Poll of the public's attitudes toward the pubic schools. *Phi Delta Kappan* 92 (1): 9–26.

Byrne, Richard. *Free technology for teachers*. http://www.freetech4teachers.com/.

California Open Source Textbook Project.
http://opensourcetext.org

Carr. N. 2008a. *The big switch: Rewiring the world, from Edison to Google.* New York: W. W. Norton & Company.

_____. 2008b. Is Google making us stupid? *The Atlantic* (July/August). http://www.theatlantic.com/magazine/archive/2008/07/is-google-making-us-stupid/6868/ (accessed June 22, 2011).

_____. 2010, July/August. Googlethink: The giant's creepy efforts to read my mind. *The Atlantic.* http://www.theatlantic.com/magazine/archive/2010/07/googlethink/8120. (accessed August 8, 2011).

Christensen, C. M., and M. B. Horn. 2010, July 12. Education as we know it is finished. *Forbes.com.* http://www.forbes.com/2010-07-12/education-online-learning-leadership-chareers-christensen.html (accessed August 10, 2011).

Comer, J. 1995. Lecture given at Education Service Center, Region IV. Houston, TX.

Common Core State Standards Initiative. 2010. *Common Core State Standards Initiative.* http://www.corestandards.org (accessed March 12, 2011).

Common Craft. 2007, May 29. *Wikis in plain English.* http://www.commoncraft.com/video-wikis-plain-english (accessed June 5, 2010).

Common Sense Media. 2011. *Common Sense Media.* http://www.commonsensemedia.org (accessed July 31, 2011).

Coyle, D. 2009. *The talent code: Greatness isn't born. It's grown. Here's how.* New York: Bantam.

Cushman, K. 2010. Show us what homework's for. *Educational Leadership* 68 (1): 74–78.

Darling-Hammond, L., R. Wei, A. Andree, N. Richardson, and S. Orphanos. 2009. *Professional learning in the learning profession: A status report on teacher development in the United States and abroad.* Stanford, CT: National Staff Development Council and The School Redesign Network at Stanford University.

Davidson, C. 2011. *Now you see it: How the brain science of attention will transform the way we live, work, and learn.* New York: Viking.

Dawkins, R. 1976. *The selfish gene.* New York: Oxford University Press.

Dehaene, S. 2009. *Reading in the brain: The science and evolution of a human invention.* New York: Viking.

Denton, P. 2007. *The power of our words: Teacher language that helps children learn.* Turner Falls, MA: Northeast Foundation for Children, Inc.

Deresiewicz, W. 2010. Solitude and leadership. *The American Scholar.* http://www.theamericanscholar.org/solitude-and-leadership/ (accessed on August 22, 2011).

DiNucci, D. 1999. Fragmented future. *Print* 32 (April): 221–222.

Doidge, N. 2007. *The brain that changes itself: Stories of personal triumph from the frontiers of brain science.* New York: Viking Penguin.

DuFour, R., and R. J. Marzano. 2011. *Leaders of learning: How district, school, and classroom leaders improve student achievement.* Bloomington, IN: Solution Tree Press.

Dweck, C. S. 2006. *Mindset: The new psychology of success.* New York: Random House.

———. 2010. Even geniuses work hard. *Educational Leadership* 68 (1): 16–20.

Emerson, R. 1849. *Nature.* Boston: Thurston, Torry, and Company.

Farrell, T. S. C. 2009. *Talking, listening, and teaching: A guide to classroom communication.* Thousand Oaks, CA: Corwin.

Fisch, K. 2007, June 22. *The Fischbowl.* http://www.thefischbowl.
blogspot.com/2007/06/did-you-know-20.html
(accessed November 9, 2010).

Ford, H. n.d. Quotation cited at Thinkexist.com. http://www.
en.thinkexist.com/quotes/henry-ford/

Foundation for Excellence in Education. 2010. *Digital learning
now!* http://www.excelined.org/DOCS/Digital%20
Learning%20Now%20Report FINAL.pdf (Accessed August
5, 2011).

Fuller, R. B. n.d. Quotation cited at Brainy Quote http://www.
brainyquote.com/quotes/authors/r/r_buckminster_fuller.
html

Gandhi, M. 1928, June. *Young India.*

Garmston, R. J., and B. M. Wellman. 2008. *The adaptive school:
A sourcebook for developing collaborative groups* (2nd ed.).
Boston: Christopher-Gordon.

Goldberg, J. 2010, November 10. The great brain books, revisted.
The Dana Foundation. http://www.dana.org/news/
cerebrum/detail.aspx?id=29284 (accessed January 7, 2011).

Goodreads. http://www.goodreads.com/.

Gray, L., N. Thomas, and L. Lewis. 2010. *Teacher's use of
educational technology in U.S. public schools: 2009.*
Washington, DC: National Center for Education Statistics,
Institute of Education Sciences, U.S. Department of
Education.

Gross, D. 2011. What the Internet is hiding from you. *CNN.* (May
19). http://www.cnn.com/2011/TECH/web/05/19/online.
privacy.pariser/index.html?hpt=Sbin
(accessed May 21, 2011).

Hart, B., and T. R. Risley. 2003. The early catastrophe. *Education
Review* 17 (1): 110–118.

Heffernan, V. 2011, August 7. Education needs a digital-age upgrade. http://opinionator.blogs.nytimes.com/2011/08/07-education-needs-a-digital-age-upgrade (accessed August 8, 2011).

Himmele, P., and W. Himmele. 2011. *Total participation techniques: Making every student an active learner*. Alexandria, VA: ASCD.

Holmes, L. 2011. The sad, beautiful fact that we're all going to miss almost everything. *NPR*. (April 18) http://www.npr.org/blogs/monkeysee/2011/04/21/135508305/the-sad-beautiful-fact-that-were-all-going-to-miss-almost-everything (accessed April 20, 2011).

Hopkins, C. 2010. Global domination: CNN iReport has now published from every country on earth. *CNN iReport*. http://www.readwriteweb.com/archives/cnns_ireport_1_country_shy_of_global_domination.php (accessed May 7, 2011).

IES National Center for Education Statistics. 2010. *Digest of Education Statistics: 2009*. NCES 2010–013 (April). http://nces.ed.gov/programs/digest/d09/ (accessed March 11, 2011).

Illinois State Board of Education. n.d. *Illinois Learning Standards: Science*. http://www.isbe.state.il.us/ils/science/standards.htm (accessed December 15, 2010).

International Reading Association. 2011. *Engage*. http://engage.reading.org (accessed May 30, 2011).

International Society for Technology in Education. 2011. *ISTE*. http://www.iste.org (accessed May 30, 2011).

iStrategy Labs. 2011. 2011 Facebook demographics and statistics: Including federal employees and gays in the military." *iStrategy Labs*. (January 3). http://www.istrategylabs.com/2011/01/2011-facebook-demographics-and-statistics-including-federal-employees-and-gays-in-the-military/ (accessed May 20, 2011).

Johnson, L., S. Adams, and K. Haywood. 2011. *The NMC Horizon Report: 2011 K–12 edition.* Austin, TX: The New Media Consortium.

Johnston, P. H. 2004. *Choice words: How our language affects children's learning.* Portland, ME: Stenhouse Publishers.

Kay, K. 2010. 21st century skills: Why they matter, what they are, and how we get there. In *21st Century Skills: Rethinking How Students Learn*, ed. J. Bellanca and R. Brandt, xiii–xxxi. Bloomington, IN: Solution Tree Press.

Knobel, M., and C. Lankshear. 2006. Discussing new literacies. *Language Arts* 84 (1): 78–86.

Knobel, M., and D. Wilber. 2009. Let's talk 2.0. *Educational Leadership* 66 (6): 20–24.

Lent, R. C. 2010. The responsibility breakthrough. *Educational Leadership* 68 (1): 68–71.

Low, J. *Pub Peeps.* http://www.facebook.com/groups/170003629693392/?ap=1.

Marzano, R. 2011. Relating to students: It's what you do that counts. *Educational Leadership* 68 (6): 82–83.

Medieval Tech Support: Norwegian Version. http://www.youtube.com/watch?v=pQHX-SigQvQ

Moss, C., and S. Brookhart. 2009. *Advancing formative assessment in every classroom: A guide for instructional leaders.* Alexandria, VA: Association for Curriculum and Supervision Development.

Nater, S., and R. Gallimore. 2006. *You haven't taught until they have learned: John Wooden's teaching principles and practices.* Morgantown, WV: Fitness Information Technology.

Northwest Educational Technology Consortium. 2005. *NETC.* http://www.netc.org/ (accessed May 30, 2011).

November, A. 2010. Technology rich, information poor. In *21st century skills: Rethinking how students learn*, eds. J. Bellanca and R. Brandt, 275–284. Bloomington, IN: Solution Tree Press.

Oran, O. 2011, June 8. *30 new android apps for 2011*. http://www.thestreet.com/story/10938476/1/5-top-android-apps-for-2011.html (accessed November 27, 2011).

Ormiston, M. 2011. *Creating a digital-rich classroom*. Bloomington, IN: Solution Tree Press.

Open Educational Resources (OER). http://www.oercommons.org

Page, S. 2007. *The difference: How the power of diversity creates better groups, firms, schools, and societies* (3rd ed.). Princeton, NJ: Princeton University Press.

Palfrey, J., and U. Gasser. 2008. *Born digital: Understanding the first generation of digital natives.* New York: Basic Books.

Pariser, E. 2011, May 3. What the internet is hiding? *Moveon.org*. www.cnn.com/2011/TECH/web/05/19/online.privacy.pariser/index.html?hpt=Sbin (accessed May 21, 2011).

Partnership for 21st Century Skills. 2004. *Partnership for 21st Century Skills*. http://www.p21.org/ (accessed June 1, 2011).

Pearson, P. D., and M. C. Gallagher. 1983. The instruction of reading comprehension. *Educational Psychology* 8:317–344.

Pink, D. 2006. *A whole new mind: Why right-brainers will rule the future*. New York: Riverhead.

Reeves, D. B. 2003. *High performance in high poverty schools: 90/90/90 and beyond.* Denver, CO: Center for Performance Assessment.

_____. 2010. The write way. *American School Board Journal* November: 46–47.

Rosen, L. D. 2010. *Rewired: Understanding the iGeneration and the way they learn.* New York: Palgrave Macmillan.

Rosenblatt, L. 1969. Towards a transactional theory of reading. *Journal of Reading Behavior* 1 (1): 31–51.

Rotherham, A., and D. Willingham. 2009. 21st century skills: The challenge ahead. *Educational Leadership* 67 (1): 16–21.

———. 2010. 21st century skills: Not new but a worthy challenge. *American Educator* (Spring):17–20.

Samuels, B. M. 2009. Can the differences between education and neuroscience be overcome by mind, brain, and education? *Mind, Brain, and Education* 3 (1): 45–55.

Schroeder, S. 2009, July 7. Facebook users are getting older. Much older. *Mashable.* http://mashable.com/2009/07/07/facebook-users-older/ (accessed May 20, 2011).

Schwartz, D. 1985. *How much is a million?* New York: HarperCollins.

Shenk, D. 2010. *The genius in all of us: Why everything you've been told about genetics, talent, and IQ is wrong.* New York: Doubleday.

Shirky, C. 2008. *Here comes everybody: The power of organizing with organization.* New York: Penguin.

Silva, E. 2010. Rebuild it and they will come. *Educational Leadership* 67 (8): 60-65.

Small, G., and G. Vorgan. 2008. *iBrain: Surviving the technological alternation of the modern mind.* New York: HarperCollins Publishers.

Sousa, D. A. (Ed.) 2010. *Mind, brain, & education: Neuroscience implications for the classroom.* Bloomington, IN: Solution Tree Press.

Tapscott, D., and A. Williams. 2006. *Wikinomics: How mass collaboration changes everything.* New York: Penguin.

Walton, G. M., and G. L. Cohen. 2011. Sharing motivation. In *Social Motivation*, ed. D. Dunning, 79–102. New York: Psychology Press.

Wappler, M. 2008. The relaunch of makeoutclub.com. *Los Angeles Times.* (July 28). http://www.latimesblogs.latimes.com/soundboard/2008/07/the-relaunch-of.html#more (accessed May 21, 2011).

Weinberger, D. 2007, June 11. The value of a man-made mess, on the Internet. *NPR.* June 11, 2007. http://www.npr.org/templates/story/story.php?storyId=10951062 (accessed November 9, 2010).

Willingham, D. 2009. *Why don't students like school? A cognitive scientist answers questions about how the mind works and what it means for the classroom.* San Francisco: John Wiley & Son.

———. 2011. *Facebook Page.* http://www.facebook.com/pages/Daniel-Willingham/56853337991.

Willis, J. 2007. Which brain research can educators trust? *Phi Delta Kappan* 88 (9): 697–699.

_____. 2008. Building a bridge from neuroscience to the classroom. *Phi Delta Kappan* 89 (6): 424–427.

_____. 2010. The current impact of neuroscience on teaching and learning. In *Mind, brain, & education: Neuroscience implications for the classroom*, ed. D. A. Sousa, 44–66. Bloomington, IN: Solution Tree Press.

Wolf, M. 2007. *Proust and the squid: The story and science of the reading brain.* New York: Harper.

Zimmer, C. 2010, December 29. 100 trillion connections: New efforts probe and map the brain's detailed architecture. *Scientific American.* http://www.scientificamerican.com/article.cfm?id=100-trillion-connections (accessed January 7, 2011).